Antiquities Discovered in the State *of* Ohio and Other Western States

Antiquities Discovered in the State *of* Ohio and Other Western States

CALEB ATWATER

With a New Introduction by
JEREMY A. SABLOFF

COMMONWEALTH BOOK COMPANY
St. Martin, Ohio

Originally published in 1820 by the
American Philosophical Society as Volume One of its
Transactions. Original pagination has been retained.

Copyright © 2022 by
Commonwealth Book Company
St. Martin, Ohio

Introduction Copyright © 1973 by
Jeremy A. Sabloff

All rights reserved. Printed in the
United States of America

ISBN: 978-1-948986-41-0

Front cover illustration:
Great Mound & Cemetery, Marietta, Ohio, circa 1840

Rear cover illustration:
Plan of the Ancient Works at Marietta, Ohio
(Charles Whittlesey, 1837)

The following introduction was written by Jeremy A. Sabloff for the 1973 edition published by AMS Press. Dr. Sabloff is currently Christopher H. Browne Distinguished Professor of Anthropology, Emeritus, at the University of Pennsylvania, and External Faculty Fellow and Past President of the Santa Fe Institute.

Caleb Atwater (1778-1867) was a lawyer who lived much of his life in Circleville, Ohio. He also was the postmaster of Circleville for many years, as well as a member of the Ohio Legislature. To historians of American archaeology, however, his most important role was that of an amateur archaeologist.

Although Atwater's professional activities kept him busy, he became interested in the local mounds and earthworks and soon expanded his investigations to the ancient mounds of the whole state of Ohio and neighboring regions. Circleville itself was founded on top of ancient earthworks, like so many other towns in Ohio such as Marietta and Newark, and was named after these remains. So, after moving to Circleville from the East in 1815, Atwater did not have to go far to find antiquities to pique his curiosity, and the study of archaeological remains quickly became his major avocation.

Atwater was one of the most important figures in the Speculative Period of American archaeology.[1] This period, which ended around 1840, marked the preprofessional era of American archaeology and was characterized by the lack of either adequate, systematic archaeological description or careful fieldwork. Along with the work of Thomas Jefferson and James McCulloh, Caleb Atwater's work presaged the trends of the later 19th century, when American archaeology came of age. Mitra, in his *History of American Anthropology*, has gone so far as to say that Caleb Atwater was the "first true archaeologist" in the Americas.[2] While this title could be debated, it can be said with some security that Atwater's study was the most important work of its time.

The descriptive sections of *Antiquities Discovered in the State of Ohio* were unparalleled in 1820 and were not surpassed until the publication of Squier and Davis's great study, *Ancient Monuments of the Mississippi Valley*, in 1848. To describe the remains he observed, Atwater employed a simple tripartite classification consisting of modern European, modern Indian, and mound builder. Only the latter were seen as the makers of the great mounds and enclosures which Atwater recorded and mapped.

While the descriptive sections were unusually good and ahead of the time, the speculative part, on the other hand, was quite typical of early 19th-century reports. A significant aspect of Atwater's work, however, is that, unlike the situation in the studies of his contemporaries, the speculations are clearly separated from the descriptions of the mounds of Ohio.

Following the racist attitude of the day, Atwater and most other writers could not believe that the mounds could have been built by native Americans or their ancestors. It was felt that the Indians were not sufficiently developed culturally to have the ability to conceive of and erect the great mounds. In order to account for the building of the mounds, a lost race of "mound builders" was postulated by many writers of the early 19th century. The lost-race hypothesis had many variants, but there was essential agreement that the mounds had been built by a civilized people of the past who had migrated away and had been replaced by the "savage" Indians. This basic hypothesis was vigorously defended by many distinguished, as well as not-too-distinguished, students of the problem throughout the 19th century. In fact, it was not until 1894, that Cyrus Thomas, with the publication of his monumental report for Major John Wesley Powell and the Bureau of Ethnology on the Bureau's mound explorations,[3] laid to rest the lost-race hypothesis once and for all among his colleagues. That is, the rising professionalism of the American archaeologists, which brought better field techniques and new, reliable data to the fore, helped to defeat the untenable racist view of native American accomplishments.[4]

Atwater believed that the mounds of Ohio and the surrounding area had been built by Hindus who had migrated to North America and the Ohio Valley, built the great mounds and enclosures, and then migrated to Mexico, where they gave rise to the high civilizations of that area. Contrary to most of his contemporaries, however, Atwater believed that the Indians had arrived on this continent before the mound builders did, and had later moved into the areas, such as Ohio, which had been vacated by the civilized mound builders.

As other scholars have noted, although Atwater's views seem somewhat outlandish to today's archaeologists, they were relatively calm and well-reasoned in comparison with some of the really far-out hypotheses of his fellow writers.[5] These latter saw all sorts of Phoenicians, Lost Tribes, and men from Atlantis, among others, involved in a complex series of historical events which led to the creation of the mounds.

It must be remembered, though, that knowledge of the temporal and spatial framework of past cultural development in the Americas was virtually nil at the time that Atwater wrote. Writers had no idea of the true chronological depth of the cultures of areas such as Ohio and had little available distributional data upon which they could base their hypotheses. It was not until well after 1914, in fact, that a secure enough time-space framework was created to enable the archaeologist to appreciate the development of the Adena (1000-300 B.C.), Hopewell (300 B.C.-A.D. 700), and Mississippian (A.D. 700-historic times) cultures of the eastern United States and to realize that Indians of all these cultures as well as some of the Indians of historic, post-contact times built mounds. Moreover, the mounds of Ohio in particular could be dated well enough so that it could be seen that most of them were built by peoples of Adena and Hopewell culture affiliations.

Finally, it should be noted that Atwater's study was originally published in 1820 by the American Antiquarian Society in the first volume of its Transactions. The Society had been founded in 1812 by Isaiah Thomas, a prominent publisher, and it counted many important intellectual and political figures among its members in the early 19th century. It also helped to promote and publish much useful archaeological work in North America. The American Antiquarian Society is still an ongoing institution today, centered in Worcester, Massachusetts, but it has given up its original interest in American archaeology, although it, along with other groups such as the American Philosophical Society, was instrumental in the development of American archaeology as a professional discipline. The publication by the Society in 1820 of Atwater's *Description of the Antiquities Discovered in the State of Ohio and Other Western States*, a descriptive landmark in the history of American archaeology, was a reflection of the major role it played in the early 19th century.

NOTES

1. See G.R. Willey, "One Hundred Years of American Archaeology," in *One Hundred Years of Anthropology*, edited by J.O. Brew, Harvard University Press, 1968, pp. 29-53, for a description of the Speculative Period.

2. P. Mitra, *A History of American Anthropology*, University of Calcutta, 1933, p. 99.

3. C. Thomas, *Report on the Mound Explorations of the Bureau of Ethnology*, Bureau of Ethnology, Washington, D.C. 1894.

4. See R. Silverberg, *Mound Builders of Ancient America: The Archaeology of a Myth*, New York Graphic Society, 1968, for a complete discussion of the rise and fall of the lost race myth.

5. See, for example, Silverberg, p. 74.

DESCRIPTION

OF THE

Antiquities

DISCOVERED IN THE

STATE OF OHIO

AND OTHER

WESTERN STATES.

COMMUNICATED TO THE

PRESIDENT OF THE AMERICAN ANTIQUARIAN SOCIETY.

BY CALEB ATWATER,

COUNSELLOR OF THE AMERICAN ANTIQUARIAN SOCIETY FOR THE STATE OF OHIO.

Illustrated by ENGRAVINGS of ANCIENT FORTIFICATIONS, MOUNDS, &c. From actual Survey.

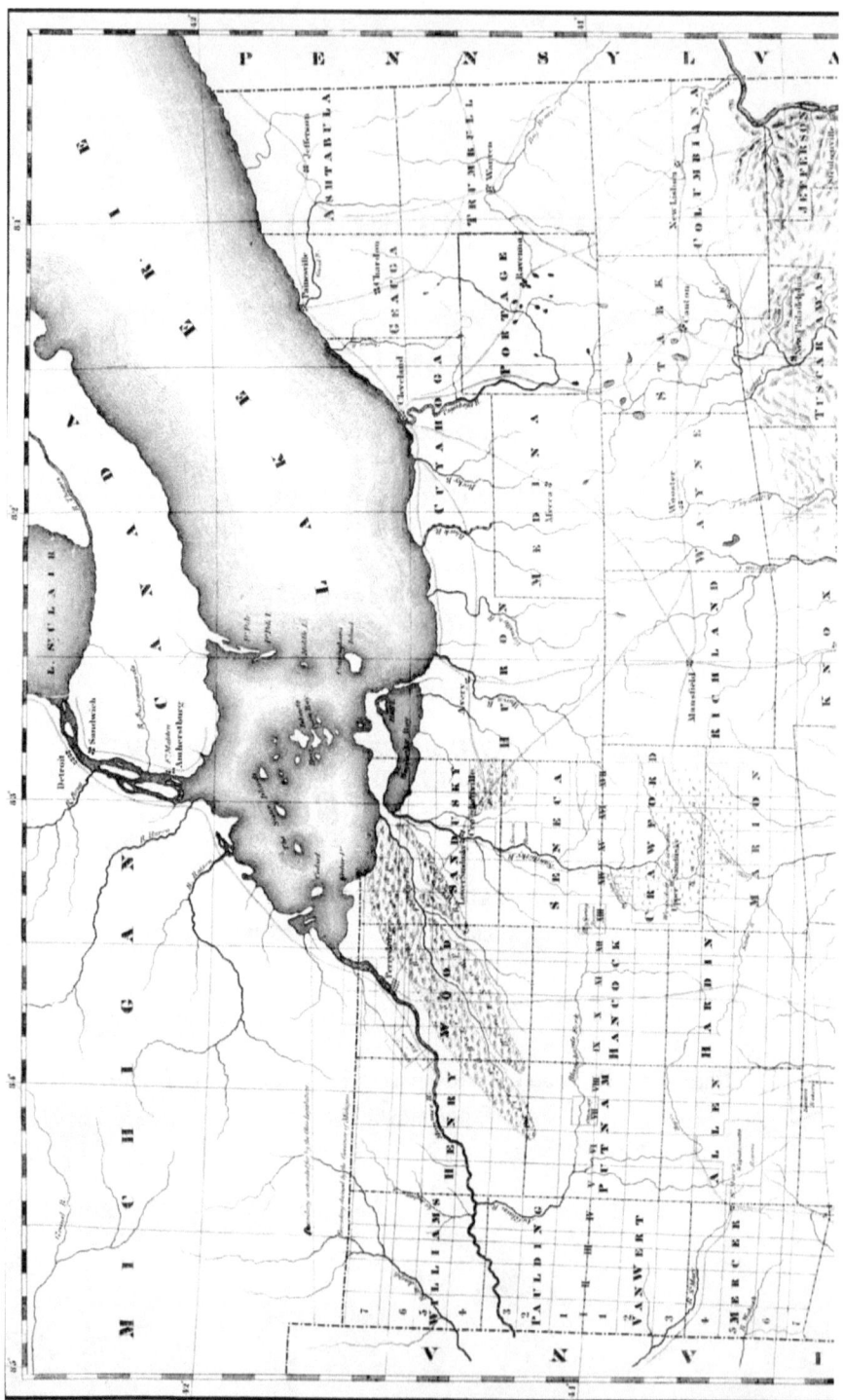

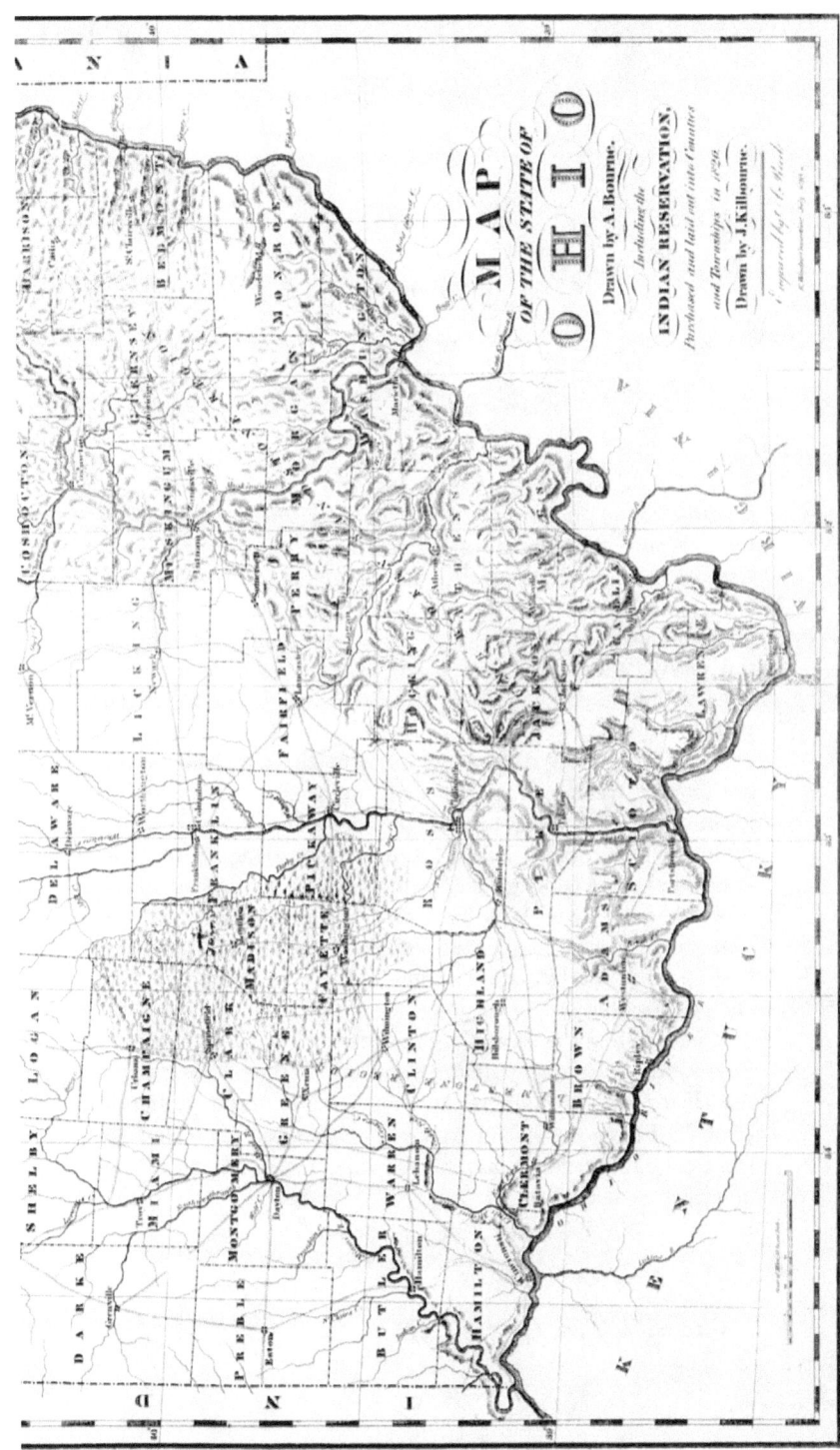

LETTER

TO THE

PRESIDENT OF THE AMERICAN ANTIQUARIAN SOCIETY.

Sir,

PERMIT me to lay before you my Memoir on the Antiquities found in the State of Ohio and the Western Country. Would that it were more worthy of the favourable notice of one, whose liberality has enabled me to complete what I had begun several years since; that my ability were equal to my zeal to serve you; that you might, in reading this essay, find a satisfaction equal to mine, whilst employed in surveying the ruins which are described in the following pages.

While traversing the country where these ancient works are found; tracing the outlines of the works; making diagram sketches of them, seated upon the summit of a lofty tumulus, which overlooked all the works belonging to some once celebrated spot, gilded by the rays of the setting sun—how anxiously have I wished for the company of some one like the person to whom these observations are addressed, so that he might participate with me in the emotions which filled my breast!

It has been my most anxious endeavour to collect and convey FACTS, which may be of some use to the Philosophers, the Historians, the Antiquarians and Divines of future times. How far I have succeeded in my humble attempt, is left to the candour, liberality and intelligence of the American Antiquarian Society.

    Sir, I am your obliged Friend,
     And very humble Servant,
         CALEB ATWATER.

Circleville, Ohio, January, 1820.

ACKNOWLEDGMENTS.

I TAKE great pleasure in acknowledging my obligations to the several Gentlemen mentioned below, for the assistance which they have rendered me, in surveying the ancient works in their immediate vicinities, &c. &c. &c.

SAMUEL WILLIAMS, Esq. Chillicothe, who surveyed the ancient works on Paint Creek, and communicated many interesting facts to me concerning our Antiquities generally.

SAMUEL P. HILDRETH, M. D. Marietta, who communicated a great number of facts concerning the Antiquities of that place, and otherwise aided me in my researches; and by these means has laid me under peculiar obligations of gratitude to him for his laudable exertions.

JOHN JOHNSTON, Esq. U. S. Indian Agent, at Piqua, furnished me, in the most obliging manner, with all the information I wished for concerning our Indians. His communications are drawn up very happily, and contain much new matter, in a condensed form.

ROSWELL MILLS, Esq. County Surveyor of Perry County, surveyed the Stone Fort in that County, and otherwise assisted me in collecting many interesting facts.

In surveying and laying down the ancient works at Portsmouth, I was assisted by Mr. JAMES ABBOT, Messrs. TRACY and PEEBLES, of that place, and WILLIAM L. MURPHY, Esq. of Chillicothe.

A. H. COFFEE, LUCIUS SMITH, and JAMES HOLMES, Esquires, surveyed the works near Newark, and shewed me every kindness, whilst I was employed in examining those interesting ruins. To them I am greatly indebted.

NEAL M'GAFFEY, Esq. Attorney at Law, of Circleville, assisted me much, as an amanuensis.

G. W. DOAN, Esq. assisted me in surveying the works at Circleville.

The services of the abovenamed Gentlemen were performed with a view to promote the good of our beloved country, and they are entitled to her gratitude.

Other Gentlemen have communicated much matter; but not being accompanied by any diagram sketches, taken from actual survey, I have thought proper not to insert it.

CALEB ATWATER.

Circleville, Ohio, January, 1820.

DESCRIPTION, &c.

OUR Antiquities have been noticed by a great number of travellers, few of whom ever saw one of them, or, who riding at full speed, had neither the industry, the opportunity, nor the ability to investigate a subject so intricate. They have frequently given to the world such crude and indigested statements, after having visited a few ancient works, or, heard the idle tales of persons incompetent to describe them, that intelligent persons residing on the very spot, would never suspect what works were intended to be described.

It has somehow happened, that one traveller has seen an ancient work, which was once a place of amusement for those who erected it, and he concludes, that none but such were ever found in the whole country. Another in his journey sees a mound of earth with a semicircular pavement on the East side of it; at once he proclaims it to the world as his firm belief, that ALL our ancient works were places of devotion, dedicated to the worship of the Sun. A succeeding tourist falls in with an ancient military fortress, and thence concludes that ALL our ancient works were raised for military purposes. One person finds something about these works of English origin, and, without hesitation, admits the supposition that they were erected by a colony of Welchmen. Others again, find articles in and near these ancient works, evidently belonging to the Indians, to people of European origin, and to that Scythian race of men who erected all our mounds of earth and stones. They find, too, articles scattered about and blended together, which belonged not only to different nations, but to different eras of time, remote from each other—they are lost in a labyrinth of doubt.— Should the inhabitants of the Western States, together with every written memorial of their existence, be swept from the face of the earth, though the difficulties of future Antiquarians would be increased, yet they would be of the same KIND with those, which now beset and overwhelm the superficial obverver.*

* His Excellency De Witt Clinton, Esq. Governour of Newyork, H. M. Brackenridge, Esq. of Baltimore, Dr. Drake, of Cincinnati, and some few others, are honourable exceptions to that class of writers above described; men of exalted talents both natural and acquired, who have attempted to describe only such works as they have carefully examined. The former gentleman has recently published "A memoir on the Antiquities of the Western Parts of Newyork." Mr. Brackenridge has examined with great care, and described with fidelity, many of the most interesting ruins of Antiquity, which are found in the Western States and Territories; whilst Dr. Drake has thrown much light on these remains, in his valuable "Picture of Cincinnati and the Miami Country." By the aid of these GREAT LAMPS, and assisted by my own *dim taper*, I have ventured to enter the heretofore dark and intricate labyrinth, where so many unfortunate travellers have lost their

Our Antiquities belong not only to different eras, in point of time, but to several nations; and those articles belonging to the same era and the same people, were intended by their authors to be applied to many different uses.

We shall divide these Antiquities into three classes. 1. Those belonging to Indians.—2. To people of European origin;—and 3. Those of that people who raised our ancient forts and tumuli.

Permit me here to premise, that in order to arrive at a result which shall be, to a certain extent, satisfactory to the candid inquirer after truth, it is necessary, not only to examine with care, and describe with fidelity, those Antiquities which are found in Ohio, but occasionally to cast a glance at those, found in other States, especially whenever they evidently, in common with ours, belong to the same people and the same era of time.

1. *Antiquities of Indians of the present race.*

Those Antiquities, which, in the strict sense of the term, belong to the North American Indians, are neither numerous nor very interesting. They consist of rude stone axes and knives, of pestles used in preparing maize for food, of arrowheads, and a few other articles so exactly similar to those found in all the Atlantic States, that a description of them

clue, and bewildered those who have undertaken to follow them. T. M. Harris, D.D. of Massachusetts, deserves honourable mention in this place. He and Dr. S. P. Hildreth of Marietta, Ohio, have described with great accuracy the Antiquities at the place last mentioned. Such writers, like the great luminary of day, give a steady light, on which we can place dependence; whilst the common herd of scribblers on this subject, resemble the ignis fatuus, which as the poet says, " leads to bewilder, and dazzles to blind."

is deemed quite useless. He who wishes to find traces of Indian settlements, either numerous, or worthy of his notice, must visit the shore of the Atlantic, or the banks of the larger rivers, emptying themselves into it, on the eastern side of the Alleghanies. The sea spreads out a continual feast before men in a savage state, little versed in the arts of civilized life, who look upon all pursuits as degrading to their dignity as men, except such as belong either to war or the chase. Having once found the ocean, there they fix their abode, and never leave it, until they are compelled to do so, by a dense population, or the overwhelming force of a powerful and victorious foe. There they cast their lines, drag their nets, or rake up the shell fishes. Into the sea, they drive the bounding roe with their dogs, and pursue him through the waves in their canoes. When they are compelled to leave the sea, they follow up the larger streams, where their finny prey abounds in every brook, and the deer, the bear, the elk, the moose, or the buffalo feeds on every hill. Whatever the earth or water spontaneously produces, they take, and are satisfied. The ocean supplied them with never failing abundance; and the wild animals, feeding in immense numbers through the fine vales and over the fertile hills of Newengland, two centuries since, were, it is believed, more numerous, than they ever were in Ohio. That species of beach which affords the nut, on which, in autumn, winter and spring, the deer and several other kinds of animals feed, thrive and fatten, was once much more abundant there, than it ever was in this State. Hence the wild animals were more numerous there than here; hence too the reason why the Indian population was more dense in the east than it was in the west. It is believed, that when America was first visited by Europeans, our prairies were too wet for the habitations of men. Besides, if our Indians came from Asia by the way of Behring's Strait, they would naturally follow down the great chain of our northwestern lakes and their outlets, nearly or quite to the sea. This may be one reason why the Indian population, at the time when our ancestors first found them there, was more dense in the northern than in the southern, in the eastern than in the western parts of the present United States. That it was so, our own history incontestably proves. Hence we deduce the reason why the cemeteries of Indians are so large and numerous in the eastern, and so small and few in the western States. Hence the numerous other traces of Indian settlements, such as the immense piles of the shells of oysters, clams, &c. all along the sea shore, the great number of arrow-heads and other articles belonging to them, in the eastern states, and their paucity here. There, we see the most indubitable evidences of the Indians having resided from very remote ages. Here, a few Indian cemeteries may be found, but they are never large, and when they are opened, ten chances to one but some article is discovered, which shows that the person has been buried since America was visited by people of European origin. An Indian's grave may frequently be known by the manner in which he was interred, which was generally in a sitting or an upright posture. Wherever we behold a number of holes in the earth, without any regard to regularity, of about a foot and a half or two feet in diameter, there by digging a few feet, we can generally find an Indian's remains. Such graves are most common along the southern shore of lake Erie, which was formerly inhabited by the Cat and Ottoway Indians. Such graves are quite common in and near the small ancient works in that part of this state. They generally interred with the deceased, something of which he had been fond in his life time; with the warriour, his battle axe; with the hunter, his bow and arrows, and that kind of wild game of which he had been the fondest, or the most successful in taking; hence the teeth of the otter are found in the grave of one, those of the bear or the beaver in another. One had been most successful in hunting the turkey, whilst another had most signalized himself by fishing. The skeleton of the turkey is found in the grave of the former; muscle shells or fishes' bones in the grave of the latter.

2. Antiquities belonging to people of European origin.

Although this division of my subject may excite a smile, when it is recollected, that three centuries have not yet elapsed since this country has been visited by Europeans, yet as articles, derived from an intercourse, which has been kept up for more than one hundred and fifty years past, between the Aborigines and several European nations are sometimes found here; and as these articles, thus derived, are frequently blended with those really very ancient, I beg leave to retain this division of Antiquities. The French were the first Europeans who traversed the territory included within the limits of the present state of Ohio. At exactly what time they *first* frequented these parts, and especially lake Erie, I have not been able to ascertain; but from authentick documents, published at Paris in the seventeenth century, we do know that they had large establishments in the territory belonging to the Six Nations, as early at least as 1655.* "A quarto volume in Latin, written by Francis Creuxieus, a jesuit, was published at Paris in 1664, and is entitled, 'Historiæ Canadeucis, seu Novæ Franciæ libri decem ad annum usque Christi MDCLVI.' It states that a French colony was established in the Onondaga territory about the year 1655, and it describes that highly interesting country: 'Ergo biduo post ingenti agmine deductus est ad locum gallorum sedi atque domicillio destinatum, leucas quatuor dissitum a pago, ubi primum pedum fixerat, bix quidquam a natura videre sit absolutius: ac si ars ut in Gallia, uteraque Europa, accederat, haud temere certaret cum Baiis. Pratum ingens cingit undique silva cædua ad ripam Lacus Gannanentæ, quo Nationes quatuor, principes Iroquoiæ totius regionis tanquam ad centrum navigolis confluere perfacile queant, et unde vicissim facillimus aditus sit ad eorum singulas, per amnes lacusque circumfluentes. Ferinæ copia certat cum copia piscium, atque ut ne desit quidquam, turtures eo indique

---

* Governour Clinton's "Memoir on the Antiquities of the western parts of Newyork."

sub veris initium convolant, tanto numero, ut reti capianter piscium quidem certe volant, ut piscatores esse feranter qui unius noctis spatium anguillas ad mille singuli, hamo capiant. Pratum intersecant fontes duo, centum prope passu salter ab altero dissiti: alterius aqua salsa salis optimi copium subministrat, alterius lympha dulcis ad potionem est; et quod mirere, uterque ex uno eademque colle scaturet.'

"It appears from Charlevoix's History of New France, that Missionaries were sent to Onondaga in 1654; that they built a chapel and made a settlement; that a French colony was established there under the auspices of Le Sieur Depuys in 1656, and retired in 1658. When La Salle started from Canada and went down the Missisippi in 1679, he discovered a large plain between the lake of the Hurons and the Illinois, in which was a fine settlement belonging to the Jesuits."*

From this time forward the French are known to have traversed that part of this state which borders on lake Erie and the Ohio river, and the larger streams which are their tributaries. Under La Salle, father Hennepin and others, they were constantly traversing this territory in their journies to and from the valley of the Missisippi. Like other Europeans of that period, they took possession of the countries which they visited, in the name of their sovereign, and, not unfrequently, left some memorial of having done so, especially in the mouths of the larger rivers and in the most remarkable ancient works. At many of the most remark-

* See Governour Clinton's Memoir.

able places which they discovered, after singing "Te Deum," they affixed the arms of France to some tree, deposited a medal in some remarkable cave, tumulus, or ancient fort, or in the mouth of some large river. Tonti, a Frenchman who accompanied La Salle in his first expedition from Canada to the Missisippi, informs us, in an account of this expedition, published at Paris in 1697, that at the mouth of the river last mentioned, the arms of France were fastened to a tree, "Te Deum" sung, formal possession of the country taken in the name of Louis XIV. and several huts built, surrounded with an intrenchment. Similar ceremonies were gone through at the mouth of the Illinois, the Wabash and Ohio, as we learn from several French travellers of that day, who published their accounts at Paris in the 17th century. Is it strange then that we should find similar medals, &c. at the mouths of other rivers, such as the great and little Miami, the Scioto, and especially the Muskingum? That medals were deposited in many places in this country, Father Hennepin, Touti, Joutel, and others, inform us; that similar medals have been found at other places is also certain.

A medal was found several years since, in the mouth of the Muskingum river, by the late Hon. Jehiel Gregory. It was a thin, round plate of lead, several inches in diameter; on one side of which, I was informed by Judge Gregory, was the French name of the river in which it lay, "Petit-belle riviere," and on the other "Louis XIV."

Near Portsmouth, a flourishing town at the mouth of the Scioto, a medal was found in alluvial earth, several years since, by a Mr. White, a number of feet below the surface, belonging, probably, to a recent era of time. This medal, I regret to state, is not in my possession, but it has been described to me by Gen. Robert Lucas and the Hon. Ezra Osborn, Esq. It was Masonick; the device on one side of it, represented a human heart with a sprig of cassia growing out of it; on the other side was a temple, with a cupola and spire, at the summit of which was a half moon, and there was a star in front of the temple. There were Roman letters on both sides of this medal, but what they were, Gen. Lucas and Judge Osborn have forgotten; they were probably abbreviations. That this medal had an European, and probably a French origin, there is little doubt, and belonged to a recent era of time.

In Trumbull county, several coins were found, not many years since, which, for a time, excited a considerable share of curiosity, until they were carefully examined by the present Governour of this state, who found that on one side of them was "George II." and on the other "Caroline," and dated in the reign of that prince.

In Harrison county, I have been credibly informed, that several coins were found, near an ancient work, evidently of European origin, belonging to a very recent era, compared with that of the ancient works where they reposed. These coins bore the name, and were dated in the reign of one of the English Charleses.

Near the mouth of Darby Creek, not far from Circleville, I have been credibly informed that a Spanish medal was found several years since, in a very good state of preservation, from which we learn that it was given by a Spanish Admiral to some person under the command of De Soto, who landed in Florida in 1538. There seems to me to be no great difficulty in accounting for such a medal being found here, near a water which runs into the Gulph of Mexico, even at such a distance from Florida, when it is recollected that a party of De Soto's men, an exploring company, which he sent out to reconnoitre the country, never returned to him nor were heard of afterwards. This medal might have been brought and lost where it was found, by the person to whom it was given, or by some Indian, who had rather have it in his own possession than in his captive's pocket.

Swords, gun barrels, knives, pickaxes, and implements of war, are often found along the banks of the Ohio, which had been left there by the French, when they had forts at Pittsburgh, Ligonier, St. Vincents, &c.

The traces of a furnace of fifty kettles, said to exist in Kentucky, a few miles in a southeastern direction from Portsmouth, appear to me to belong to the same era, and owe their origin to the same people.

Several Roman coins, said to have been found in a cave near Nashville, in Tennessee, bearing date not many centuries after the Christian era, have excited some interest among Antiquarians. They were either discovered where the finder had purposely lost them, or, what is more probable, had been left there by some European since this country was traversed by the French.

That a Frenchman should be in possession of a few Roman coins, and that he should deposit them in some remarkable cave which he chanced to visit in his travels, is not surprising. That some persons have *purposely* lost coins, medals, &c. &c. in caves which they knew were about to be explored; or deposited them in tumuli, which they knew were about to be opened, is a well known fact, which has occurred at several places in this western country.

In one word, I will venture to assert, that there never has been found a medal, coin, or monument, in all North America, which had on it one or more letters, belonging to any alphabet, now or ever in use among men of any age or country, that did not belong to Europeans or their descendants, and had been brought or made here since the discovery of America by Christopher Columbus.

3. *Antiquities of the People who formerly inhabited the Western Parts of the United States.*

It is time to consider the third, last, and most highly interesting class of Antiquities, which comprehends those belonging to that people who erected our ancient forts and tumuli; those military works, whose walls and ditches cost so much labour in their structure, those numerous and sometimes lofty mounds, which owe their origin to a people far more civilized than our Indians, but far less so than Europeans. These works are interesting, on many accounts, to the Antiquarian, the Philosopher, and the Divine, especially when we consider the immense extent of country which they cover; the great labour which they cost their authors; the acquaintance with the useful arts, which that people had, when compared with our present race of Indians; the grandeur of many of the works themselves; the total absence of all historical records, or even traditionary accounts respecting them; the great interest which the learned have taken in them; the contradictory and erroneous accounts which have generally been given of them; to which we may add, the destruction of them which is going on in almost every place where they are found in this whole country, have jointly contributed to induce me to bestow no inconsiderable share of attention to this class of Antiquities. They were once forts, cemeteries, temples, altars, camps, towns, villages, race grounds, and other places of amusement, habitations of chieftains, videttes, watch towers, monuments, &c. These ancient works, especially the mounds, both of earth and stone, are found in every quarter of the habitable globe.

In what Parts of the World ancient Works of this kind are found.

These ancient works, so much talked about, and so little understood, are spread over an immense extent of country, in Europe and the northern parts of Asia. They may be traced from Wales to Scotland on the island of Britain;—they are found in Ireland, in Normandy, in France, in Sweden, and quite across the Russian empire, to our continent. In Africa we see pyramids, which derive their origin from the same source. In Judea, and throughout all Palestine, works similar to ours exist. In Tartary they abound in all the steppes. I know not whether Lewis and Clarke saw any of these works on Columbia river; but they did not traverse that country by land, and had of course but little opportunity to discover them, if there. But on this side of the Rocky Mountains they did see them frequently; and I have little doubt of their existing all the way, from the spot where, we are informed, the ark of Noah rested, to our northwestern lakes, down them and their outlets, as far as the Black River country, on the southern shore of lake Ontario in Newyork.

On the south side of Ontario, one not far from Black River, is the farthest in a northeastern direction on this continent. One on the Chenango river, at Oxford, is the farthest south, on the eastern side of the Alleghanies. These works are small, very ancient, and appear to mark the utmost extent of the settlement of the people who erected them in that direction. Coming from Asia, finding our great lakes, and following them down thus far, Were they driven back by the ancestors of our Indians? and, Were the small forts above alluded to, built in order to protect them from the aborigines who had before that time settled along the Atlantick coast? In travelling towards lake Erie, in a western direction from the works above mentioned, a few small works are occasionally found, especially in Genesee county; but they are few and small, until we arrive at the mouth of Catarangus creek, a water of lake Erie, in Catarangus county, in the state of Newyork, where Governour Clinton, in his " Memoir &c."

says a line of forts commences, extending south upwards of fifty miles, and not more than four or five miles apart. There is said to be another line of them parallel to these, which generally contain a few acres of ground only, whose walls are only a few feet in height. For an able account of the Antiquities in the western parts of Newyork, we must again refer to Governour Clinton's Memoir, not wishing to repeat what he has so well said.

If the works already alluded to, are real forts, they must have been built by a people few in number, and quite rude in the arts of life. Travelling towards the southwest, these works are frequently seen, but like those already mentioned, they are comparatively small, until we arrive on the Licking near Newark, where are some of the most extensive and intricate, as well as interesting, of any in this state, perhaps in the world. Leaving these, still proceeding in a southwestern direction, we find some very extensive ones at Circleville. At Chillicothe there were some, but the destroying hand of man has despoiled them of their contents, and entirely removed them. On Paint Creek are some, far exceeding all others in some respects, where probably was once an ancient city of great extent. At the mouth of the Scioto, are some very extensive ones, as well as at the mouth of the Muskingum. In fine, these works are thickly scattered over the vast plain from the southern shore of lake Erie, to the Mexican Gulph, increasing in number, size and grandeur as we proceed towards the south. They may be traced around the Gulph, across the province of Texas into Newmexico, and all the way into South America. They abound most in the vicinity of good streams, and are never, or rarely found, except in a fertile soil. They are not found in the prairies of Ohio, and rarely in the barrens, and there they are small, and situated on the edge of them, and on dry ground. From the Black River country in Newyork, to this state, I need say no more concerning them; but at Salem in Ashtabula county, there is one on a hill, which merits a few words, though it is a small one compared with others farther south. The work at Salem, is on a hill near Coneaught river, if my information be correct, and is about three miles from lake Erie. It is round, having two parallel circular walls, and a ditch between them. Through these walls, leading into the inclosure, are a gateway and a road, exactly like a modern turnpike, descending down the hill to the stream by such a gradual slope, that a team with a waggon might easily either ascend or descend it, and there is no other place by which these works could be approached, without considerable difficulty. Within the bounds of this ancient enclosure, the trees which grew there were such as denote the richest soil in this country, while those growing on the outside of these ruins, were such as denote the poorest.

On the surface of the earth, within this circular work, and immediately below it, pebbles rounded, and having their angles worn off in water, such as are now seen on the present shore of the lake, are found; but they are represented as bearing visible marks of having been burned in a hot fire. Bits of earthen ware, of a coarse kind, and of a rude structure, without any glazing, are found here on the surface, and a few inches below it. This ware is represented to me as having been manufactured of sand stone and clay. My informant says, within this work are sometimes found skeletons of a people of small stature, which, if true, sufficiently identifies it to have belonged to that race of men who erected our tumuli. The vegetable mould covering the surface within the works, is at least ten inches in depth. In these same works have been found articles, evidently belonging to Indians, of their own manufacture, as well as others, which they had derived from their intercourse with Europeans and their descendants. I mention the fact here, thus particularly, in order to save the repetition of it in describing nearly every work of this kind, especially along the shore of lake Erie, and the banks of the larger rivers. This circumstance I wish the reader to keep in mind. Indian Antiquities are always either on, or a very small distance below, the surface, unless buried in some grave; whilst articles, evidently belonging to that people who raised our mounds, are frequently found many feet below the surface, especially in river bottoms.

Still proceeding in a southwestern direction, there are, at different places, several small ancient works, scattered over the country, some in regular forms, and others appear to have been thrown up to suit the ground where they are situated; but their walls are only a few feet in height, encompassing, generally, but a few acres, with ditches of no great depth, evidently shewing the population to have been inconsiderable.

I have been informed, that in the north part of Medina county, Ohio, there are some works, near one of which, a piece of marble well polished, was lately found. It might have been a composition of clay and sulphat of lime or plaster of Paris, such as I have often seen in and about ancient works along the Ohio river. A common observer would mistake the one for the other, which I am disposed to believe was the case here.

Ancient Works *near* NEWARK, Ohio.

Proceeding still to the southward, the ancient works become more and more numerous, and more intricate, and of greater size; denoting the increase of their authors, in number, strength, and a better acquaintance with the art of constructing them. At length we reach the interesting ones on two branches of the Licking, near Newark, in Licking county, Ohio, which, on many accounts, are quite as remarkable as any others in North America, or, perhaps in any part of the world.

By referring to the scale on which they are projected, it will be seen that these works are of great extent. [*See the Plate.*]

A. is a fort containing about forty acres, within its walls, which are, generally, I should judge, about ten feet in height. Leading into this, fort are 8 openings or gateways, about fifteen feet in width; in front of which, is a small mound of earth, in height and thickness resembling the outer wall. [*See m, m, m, m, m, m, m.*] These small mounds are about four feet longer than the gateway is in width; otherwise they look as if the wall had been moved

ANCIENT WORKS, near Newark in LICKING COUNTY: OHIO.

Scale of Chains.

REFERENCES.

A. a Fort nearly in form of an octagon.
B. a Round Fort connected with the former by parallel walls.
C. a Round Fort with a ditch around it.
D. a Square Fort.
E. a Pond containing 150 acres or upwards.
I. Supposed to have been cultivated fields.
c. Parallel walls of earth.
a. Small works of defence.
b. Pass down to the water.
m. Small mounds for the defence of the gates in the octagonal Fort.
d. an Observatory, partly of snow, 18 feet high.
CD. Two parallel walls, surveyed on a mile or two, their total length unknown.
G. a Steep declivity 80 feet nearly perpendicular.
F. Alluvion formed since these works were deserted.

Engraved for the American Antiquarian Society.

PLATE II.

into the fort eight or ten feet. These small mounds of earth were probably intended for the defence of the gates, opposite to which they are situated. The walls of this work, consisting of earth, are taken from the surface so carefully and uniformly, that it cannot now be discovered from what spot. They are as nearly perpendicular as the earth could be made to lie.

B. is a round fort, containing twentytwo acres, connected with *A.* by two parallel walls of earth of about the same height, &c. as those of *A.* At *d.* is an OBSERVATORY, built partly of earth and partly of stone. It commanded a full view of a considerable part, if not all the plain, on which these ancient works stand; and would do so now, were the thick growth of ancient forest trees, which clothe this tract, cleared away. Under this observatory, was a passage, from appearances, and a secret one probably, to the water course which once run near this spot, but has since moved farther off.

C. is a circular fort, containing about twentysix acres, having a wall around it, which was thrown out of a deep ditch on the inner side of the wall. This wall is now from twentyfive to thirty feet in height; and when I saw this work, the ditch was half filled with water, especially on the side towards *E.* There are parallel walls of earth, *c, c, c, c, c, c,* generally five or six rods apart, and four or five feet in height. Their extent may be measured by the reader, by referring to the scale annexed to the plates.

D. is a square fort, containing twenty acres, whose walls are similar to those of *A.*

E, is a pond, covering from one hundred and fifty to two hundred acres; which was a few years since entirely dry, so that a crop of Indian corn was raised where the water is now ten feet in depth, and appears still to be rising. This pond sometimes reaches to the very walls of *C.* and to the parallel walls towards its northern end.

F, F, F, F, is the interval, or alluvion, made by the Racoon and south fork of Licking river, since they washed the foot of the hill at *G, G, G.* When these works were occupied, we have reason to believe that these streams washed the foot of this hill, and as one proof of it, passages down to the water have been made of easy ascent and descent at *b, b, b, b.*

G, G, G, an ancient bank of the creeks, which have worn their channels considerably deeper than they were when they washed the foot of this hill. These works stand on a large plain, which is elevated forty or fifty feet above the interval *F, F, F.* and is almost perfectly flat, and as rich a piece of land as can be found in any country. The reader will see the passes, where the authors of these works entered into their fields at *I, I, I, I, I.* and which were probably cultivated. The watch towers, *a, a, a, a,* were placed at the ends of parallel walls, or ground as elevated as could be found on this extended plain. They were surrounded by circular walls, now only four or five feet in height. It is easy to see the utility of these works, placed at the several points where they stand.

C. D. two parallel walls, leading probably to other works, but not having been traced more than a mile or two, are not laid down even as far as they were surveyed.

The high ground, near Newark, appears to have been the place, and the only one which I saw, where the ancient occupants of these works buried their dead, and even these tumuli appeared to me to be small. Unless others are found in the vicinity, I should conclude, that the original owners, though very numerous, did not reside here during any great length of time. I should not be surprized if the parallel walls *C. D.* are found to extend from one work of defence to another, for the space of thirty miles, all the way across to the Hockhocking, at some point a few miles north of Lancaster. Such walls having been discovered at different places, probably belonging to these works, for ten or twelve miles at least, leads me to suspect that the works on Licking, were erected by people who were connected with those who lived on the Hockhocking river, and that their road between the two settlements was between these parallel walls.

If I might be allowed to conjecture the use to which these works were originally put, I should say, that the larger works were really military ones of defence; that their authors lived within the walls; that the parallel walls were intended for the double purposes of protecting persons in times of danger, from being assaulted while passing from one work to another; and they might also serve as fences, with a very few gates, to fence in and enclose their fields, at *I, I, I, I.* as the plate will show.

The hearths, burnt charcoal, cinders, wood, ashes, &c. which were uniformly found in all similar places, that are now cultivated, have not been discovered here; this plain being probably an uncultivated forest. I found here, several arrow heads, such as evidently belonged to the people, who raised other similar works.

The care which is every where visible, about these ruins, to protect every part from a foe without; the high plain on which they are situated, which is generally forty feet above the country around it; the pains taken to get at the water, as well as to protect those who wished to obtain it; the fertile soil, which appears to me to have been cultivated, are circumstances not to be overlooked; they speak volumes in favour of the sagacity of their authors.

A few miles below Newark, on the south side of the Licking, are some of the most extraordinary holes, dug in the earth, for number and depth, of any within my knowledge, which belonged to the people we are treating of. In popular language, they are called "wells," but were not dug for the purpose of procuring water, either fresh or salt.

There are at least a thousand of these "*wells;*" many of them are now more than twenty feet in depth. A great deal of curiosity has been excited, as to the objects sought for, by the people who dug these holes. One gentleman nearly ruined himself, by digging in and about these works, in quest of the precious metals; but he found nothing very precious. I have been at the pains to obtain specimens of all the minerals, in and near these wells. They have not all of them been put to proper tests; but I can say, that rock crystals, some of them very beautiful, and horn stone, suitable for arrow and spear heads, and a little lead, sulphur, and iron, was all that I could ascertain correctly to belong to the specimens in my possession. Rock crystals, and stone arrow and spear heads, were in great repute among them, if we are to judge from the numbers of them, found in such of the mounds as were common cemeteries. To a rude people, nothing would stand a better chance of being esteemed, as an ornament, than such a stone.

On the whole, I am of the opinion, that these holes were dug for the purpose of procuring the articles above named; and that it is highly probable, a vast population once *here*, procured these, in their estimation, highly ornamental and useful articles. And it is possible that they might have procured some lead here, though by no means probable, because we no where find any lead which ever belonged to them, and it will not very soon, like iron, become an oxyde, by rusting.

Ancient Works in PERRY COUNTY, Ohio.

Southwardly from the great works on the Licking, four or five miles in a northwestern direction from Somerset, the seat of justice for Perry county, and on section twentyone, township seven, range sixteen, is an ancient work of stone. [*See the plate.*]

A. is the area of this work. *M.* a stone mound near the centre of it. This stone mound is circular, and in form of a sugar loaf, from twelve to fifteen feet in height. There is a smaller circular stone tumulus

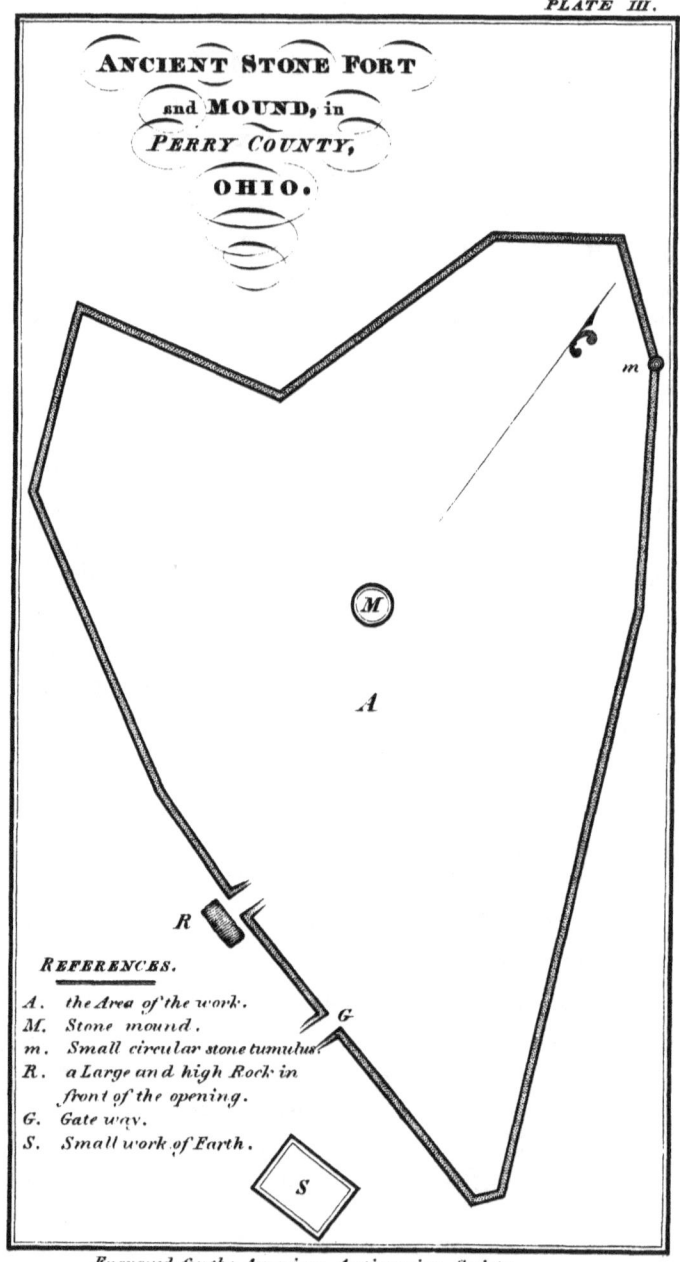

at *m.* standing in the wall, which encloses the work, and constituting a part of it.

R. is a large and high rock, lying in front of an opening in the outer wall. This opening is a passage between two large rocks, which lie in the wall, of from seven to ten feet in width. These rocks, on the outside, present a perpendicular front of ten feet in altitude, but after extending fifty yards into the enclosure, they enter the earth and disappear. There is a gateway at *G.* much as is represented in the plate.

S. is a small work, whose area is half an acre; the walls are of earth, and of a few feet only in height. This large stone work contains within its walls forty acres and upwards. The walls, as they are called in popular language, consist of rude fragments of rocks, without any marks of any iron tool upon them. These stones lie in the utmost disorder, and if laid up in a regular wall, would make one seven feet or seven feet six inches in height, and from four to six feet in thickness. I do not believe this ever to have been a military work, either of defence or offence; but if a military work, it must have been a temporary camp. From the circumstance of this work's containing two stone tumuli, such as were used in ancient times, as altars and as monuments, for the purpose of perpetuating the memory of some great era, or important event in the history of those who raised them, I should rather suspect this to have been a sacred enclosure, or "high place," which was resorted to on some great anniversary. It is on high ground, and destitute of water, and of course, could not have been a place of habitation for any length of time. It might have been the place, where some solemn feast was annually held by the tribe by which it was formed. The place has become a forest, and the soil is too poor to have ever been cultivated by a people who invariably chose to dwell on a fertile spot. These monuments of ancient manners, how simple and yet how sublime. Their authors were rude, and unacquainted with the use of letters, yet they raised monuments, calculated almost for endless duration, and speaking a language as expressive as the most studied inscriptions of latter times upon brass and marble. These monuments, their stated anniversaries and traditionary accounts, were their means of perpetuating the recollection of important transactions. Their authors are gone; their monuments remain; but the events, which they were intended to keep in the memory, are lost in oblivion.

Ancient Works at MARIETTA, Ohio.

Having already described several ancient works, either on or near the waters of the Muskingum, I shall trace them down that river. But there are none of any considerable note, except those on the Licking, which falls into that stream at Zanesville, until we arrive at some, situated near its banks in Morgan county, which, however, have not been surveyed. These are mounds of earth and stones, and their description is reserved, until we arrive at that part of this memoir, which will be devoted to a consideration of that class of Antiquities.

Proceeding down the Muskingum to its mouth, at Marietta, are some of the most extraordinary ancient works, any where to be found. They have been often examined, and as often very well described; yet as some additional facts have come to my knowledge, and as other works in many parts of the western country are similar to them; and as comparisons ought to be instituted between works evidently of the same class, I have ventured to collect together a mass of facts concerning them, derived from several intelligent persons, who have published their statements, as well as some from others who have obligingly laid before me additional information.

Manasseh Cutler, LL. D. many years since, published an accurate account of these works. Next followed " The Journal of a Tour" into this country, by Thaddeus M. Harris, D. D. in which may be found much useful information concerning them, accompanied by a diagram sketch of them, very accurately drawn from actual survey, by Gen. Rufus Putnam, of Marietta. I have carefully compared these well written accounts with those which I have received from Dr. S. P. Hildreth, of Marietta, Gen. Edward W. Tupper, of Gallipolis, and several other gentlemen residing on the Ohio.— From these highly respectable sources, I have drawn my information. These works have been more fortunate than many others of this kind in North America; no despoiling hand has been laid upon them; and no blundering, hasty traveller has, to my knowledge, pretended to describe them. The mound which was used as a cemetery is entire, standing in the burying ground of the present town. Cutler, Putnam and Harris are intelligent men.

It will be seen that I have quoted largely from Drs. Cutler and Harris; not, however, without first ascertaining that their accounts were perfectly correct, as to all the *facts* which they have stated.

*" The situation of these works is on an elevated plain, above the present bank of the Muskingum, on the east side, and about half a mile from its junction with the Ohio. They consist of walls and mounds of earth, in direct lines, and in square and circular forms.

" The largest square fort, by some called the town, contains 40 acres, encompassed by a wall of earth, from 6 to 10 feet high, and from 25 to 36 feet in breadth at the base. On each side are three openings, at equal distances, resembling 12 gateways. The entrances at the middle, are the largest, particularly on the side next to the Muskingum. From this outlet is a covert way, formed of two parallel walls of earth, 231 feet distant from each other, measuring from centre to centre. The walls at the most elevated part, on the inside, are 21 feet in height, and 42 in breadth at the base, but on the outside average only five feet in height. This forms a passage of about 360 feet in length, leading by a gradual descent to the low grounds, where, at the time of its construction, it probably reached the river. Its walls commence at 60 feet from the ramparts of the fort, and increase in elevation as the way descends towards the river; and the bottom is crowned in the

* Harris's Tour, page 149.

centre, in the manner of a well founded turnpike road.

"Within the walls of the fort, at the northwest corner, is an oblong elevated square, 188 feet long, 132 broad, and nine feet high; level on the summit, and nearly perpendicular at the sides. At the centre of each of the sides, the earth is projected, forming gradual ascents to the top, equally regular, and about six feet in width. Near the south wall is another elevated square, 150 feet by 120, and eight feet high, similar to the other, excepting that instead of an ascent to go up on the side next the wall, there is a hollow way 10 feet wide, leading 20 feet towards the centre, and then rising with a gradual slope to the top. At the southeast corner is a third elevated square, 108 by 54 feet, with ascents at the ends, but not so high nor perfect as the two others. A little to the southwest of the centre of the fort is a circular mound, about 30 feet in diameter and five feet high, near which are four small excavations at equal distances, and opposite each other. At the southwest corner of the fort is a semicircular parapet, crowned with a mound, which guards the opening in the wall. Towards the southeast, is a smaller fort, containing 20 acres, with a gateway in the centre of each side and at each corner. These gateways are defended by circular mounds.

"On the outside of the smaller fort is a mound, in form of a sugar loaf, of a magnitude and height which strike the beholder with astonishment. Its base is a regular circle, 115 feet in diameter; its perpendicular altitude is 30 feet. It is surrounded by a ditch four feet deep and 15 feet wide, and de-

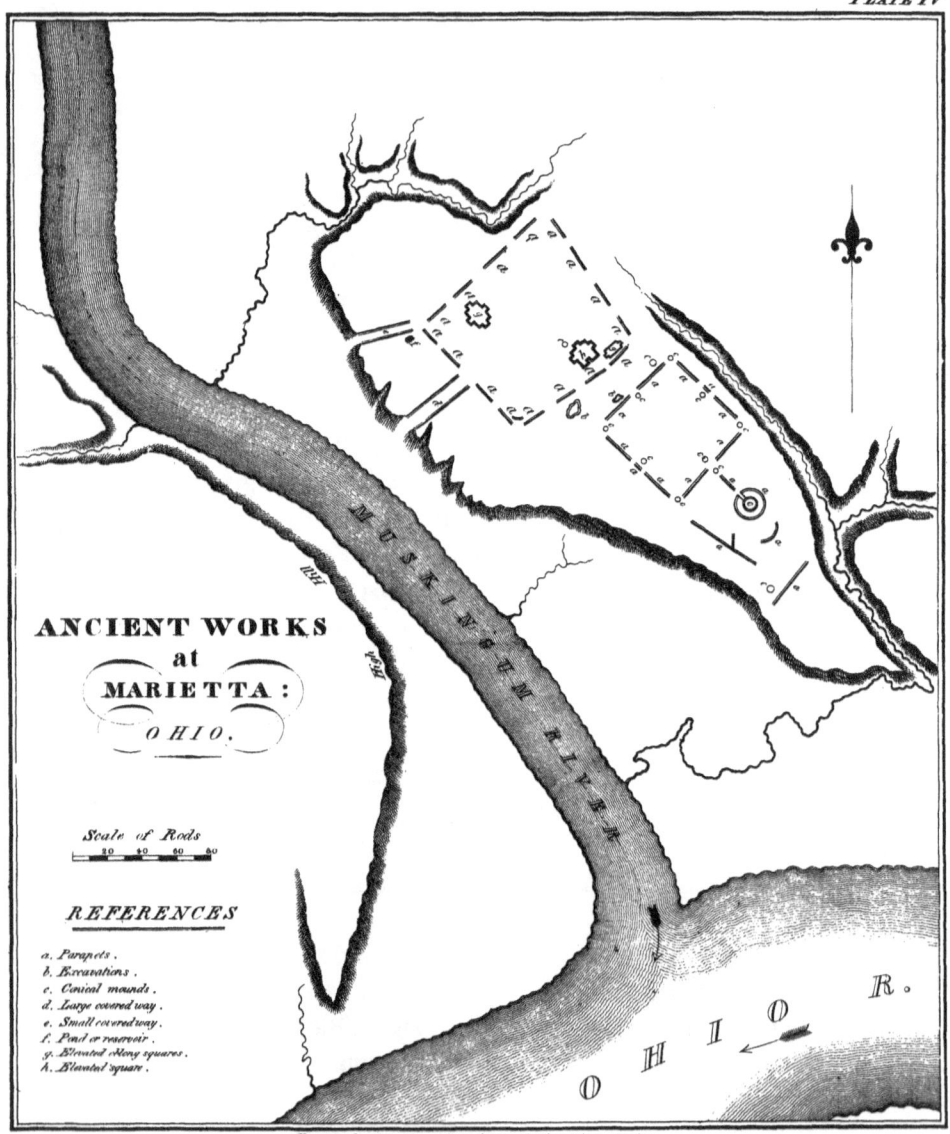

fended by a parapet four feet high, through which is a gateway towards the fort, 20 feet in width. There are other walls, mounds, and excavations less conspicuous and entire, which will be best understood by referring to the annexed drawings."

Some additional particulars respecting these works, are contained in the following extracts from a letter, written by Dr. S. P. Hildreth, of Marietta, to the author, dated 8th June, 1819.

" Mr. Harris, in his ' *Tour*,' has given a tolerably good account of the present appearance of the works, as to height, shape and form. (I must refer you to this work.) The principal excavation, or well, is as much as 60 feet in diameter, at the surface; and when the settlement was first made, it was at least 20 feet deep. It is at present, 12 or 14 feet; but has been filled up a great deal from the washing of the sides by frequent rains. It was originally of the kind formed in the most early days, when the water was brought up by hand in pitchers, or other vessels, by steps formed in the sides of the well.

" The pond, or reservoir, near the northwest corner of the large fort, was about 25 feet in diameter, and the sides raised above the level of the adjoining surface by an embankment of earth three or four feet high. This was nearly full of water at the first settlement of the town, and remained so until the last winter, at all seasons of the year. When the ground was cleared near the well, a great many logs that laid nigh, were rolled into it, to save the trouble of piling and burning them. These, with the annual deposit of leaves, &c. for ages, had filled the well nearly full; but still the water rose to the surface, and had the appearance of a stagnant pool. In early times, poles and rails have been pushed down into the water, and deposit of rotten vegetables, to the depth of 30 feet. Last winter the person who owns the well, undertook to drain it, by cutting a ditch from the well into the *small " covert way;"* and he has dug to the depth of about 12 feet, and let the water off to that distance. He finds the sides of the reservoir not perpendicular, but projecting gradually towards the centre of the well, in the form of an inverted cone. The bottom and sides, so far as he has examined, are lined with a stratum of very fine, ash coloured clay, about 8 or 10 inches in thickness; below which, is the common soil of the place, and above it, this vast body of decayed vegetation. The proprietor calculates to take from it several hundred loads of excellent manure, and to continue to work at it, until he has satisfied his curiosity, as to the depth and contents of the well. If it was actually a well, it probably contains many curious articles, which belonged to the ancient inhabitants.

"On the outside of the parapet, near the *oblong square*, I picked up a considerable number of fragments of ancient potters' ware. This ware is ornamented with lines, some of them quite curious and ingenious, on the outside. It is composed of clay and fine gravel, and has a partial glazing on the inside. It seems to have been burnt, and capable of holding liquids. The fragments, on breaking them, look quite black, with brilliant particles, appearing as you hold them to the light. The ware which I have seen, found near the rivers, is composed of shells and clay, and not near so hard as this found on the plain. It is a little curious, that of 20 or 30 pieces which I picked up, nearly all of them were found on the outside of the parapet, as if they had been thrown over the wall purposely. This is, in my mind, strong presumptive evidence, that the parapet was crowned with a palisade. The chance of finding them on the inside of the parapet, was equally good, as the earth had been recently ploughed, and planted with corn. Several pieces of copper have been found in and near to the ancient works, at various times. One piece, from the description I had of it, was in the form of a cup with low sides, the bottom very thick and strong. The small mounds in this neighbourhood have been but slightly, if at all examined.

"The avenues, or places of ascent on the sides of the elevated squares, are ten feet wide, instead of six, as stated by Mr. Harris. His description, as to height and dimensions, are otherwise correct.

"There was lately found at Waterford, not far from the bank of the Muskingum, a magazine of spear and arrow heads, sufficient to fill a peck measure. They laid in one body, occupying a space of about eight inches in width and 18 in length, and at one end about a foot from the surface of the earth, and 18 inches at the other; as though they had been buried in a box, and one end had sunk deeper in the earth than the other. They were found by Mr. B. Dana of Waterford, as he was digging the earth to remove a large pear tree. The spot was formerly covered by a house, in the early settlement of the place. They appear never to have been used, and are of various lengths from six to two inches; they have no shanks, but are in the shape of a triangle, with two long sides, thus ▷."

It is worthy of remark, that the walls and mounds were not thrown up from ditches, but raised by bringing the earth from a distance, or taking it up uniformly from the plain; resembling, in that respect, most of the ancient works at Licking, already described. It has excited some surprize that the tools have not been discovered here, with which these works were constructed. Those who have examined these ruins, seem not to have been aware, that with shovels made of wood, earth enough to have constructed these works might have been taken from the surface, with as much ease, almost, as if they were made of iron. This will not be as well understood on the east as the west side of the Alleghanies; but those who are acquainted with the great depth and looseness of our vegetable mould, which lies on the surface of the earth, and of course, the ease with which it may be raised by wooden tools, will cease to be astonished at what would be an immense labour in what geologists call "primitive" countries. Besides, had the people who raised these works, been in possession of, and used ever so many tools, manufactured from iron, by lying either on or under the earth, during all that long period which has intervened between their authors and us, they would have long since oxydized by "rusting," and left but faint traces of their existence behind them.

Ancient Works *at* CIRCLEVILLE, Ohio.

Having noticed the principal works of this kind on the waters of the Muskingum, we shall next consider those which might have once been military works on the waters of the Scioto.

From near Lower Sandusky, I am not informed of any worthy of notice, that is, "FORTS," until we arrive at Circleville, 26 miles south of Columbus.

These are situated not far from the junction of Hargus's creek with the latter river, which is on the east side of the river, and south side of the creek. By referring to the plate, the reader will be better enabled to understand the description which follows.

There are two forts, one being an exact circle, the other an exact square. The former is surrounded by two walls, with a deep ditch between them. The latter is encompassed by one wall, without any ditch. The former was 69 feet in diameter, measuring from outside to outside of the circular outer wall; the latter is exactly 55 rods square measuring the same way. The walls of the circular fort were at least 20 feet in height, measuring from the bottom of the ditch, before the town of Circleville was built. The inner wall was of clay, taken up probably in the northern part of the fort, where was a low place, and is still considerably lower than any other part of the work. The outside wall was taken from the ditch which is between these walls, and is alluvial, consisting of pebbles worn smooth in water, and sand, to a very considerable depth, more than 50 feet at least. The outside

PLATE V

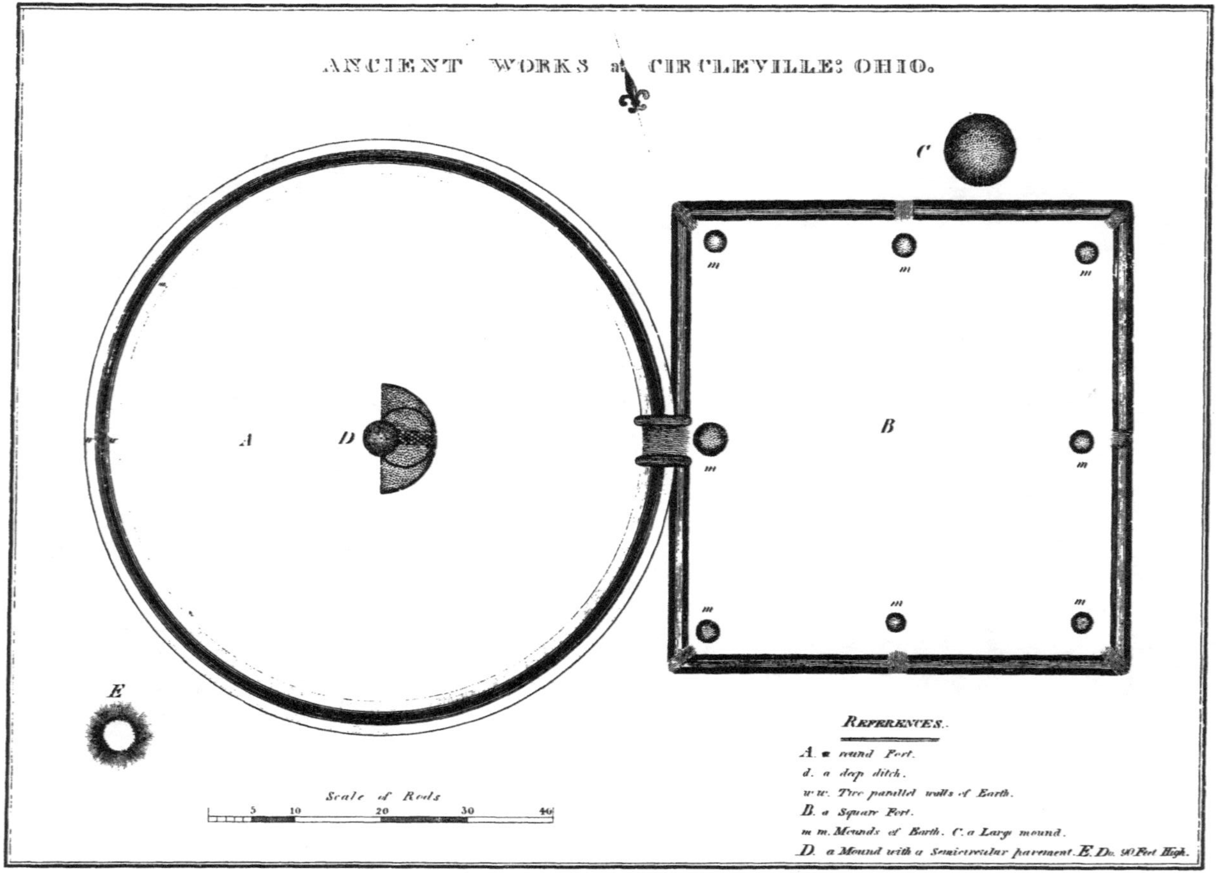
ANCIENT WORKS at CIRCLEVILLE: OHIO.
A
D
B
C
E
m
Scale of Rods
5
10
20
30
40
REFERENCES.
A. a round Fort.
d. a deep ditch.
w w. Two parallel walls of Earth.
B. a Square Fort.
m m. Mounds of Earth. C. a Large mound.
D. a Mound with a Semicircular pavement. E. Do. 90 Feet High.

Engraved for the American Antiquarian Society.

of the walls is about five or six feet in height now; on the inside, the ditch is, at present, generally not more than 15 feet. They are disappearing before us daily, and will soon be gone. The walls of the square fort, are, at this time, where left standing, about 10 feet in height. There were eight gateways, or openings, leading into the square fort, and only one into the circular fort. Before each of these openings was a mound of earth, perhaps four feet high, 40 feet perhaps in diameter at the base, and 20 or upwards at the summit. These mounds, for two rods or more, are exactly in front of the gateways, and were intended for the defence of these openings.

As this work was a perfect square, so the gateways and their watch towers were equidistant from each other. These mounds were in a perfectly straight line, and exactly parallel with the wall.— Those small mounds were at *m, m, m, m, m, m, m*. The black line at *d*, represents the ditch, and *w, w*, represent the two circular walls.

D. [The reader is referred to the plate.] Shows the scite of a once very remarkable ancient mound of earth, with a semicircular pavement on its eastern side, nearly fronting, as the plate represents, the only gateway leading into this fort. This mound is entirely removed; but the outline of the semicircular pavement, may still be seen in many places, notwithstanding the dilapidations of time, and those occasioned by the hand of man. This mound, the pavement, the walk from the east to its elevated summit, the contents of the mound, &c. will be described under the head of mounds.

The earth in these walls was as nearly perpendicular as it could be made to lie. This fort had originally but one gateway leading into it on its eastern side, and that was defended by a mound of earth, several feet in height, at *m. i.* Near the centre of this work, was a mound, with a semicircular pavement on its eastern side, some of the remains of which may still be seen by an intelligent observer. The mound at *m. i.* has been entirely removed, so as to make the street level, from where it once stood.

B. is a square fort, adjoining the circular one, as represented by the plate, the area of which has been stated already. The wall which surrounds this work, is generally, now, about 10 feet in height, where it has not been manufactured into brick.— There are seven gateways leading into this fort, besides the one which communicates with the square fortification, that is, one at each angle, and another in the wall, just half way between the angular ones. Before each of these gateways was a mound of earth of four or five feet in height, intended for the defence of these openings.

The extreme care of the authors of these works to protect and defend every part of the circle, is no where visible about this square fort. The former is defended by two high walls; the latter by one. The former has a deep ditch encircling it; this has none. The former could be entered at one place only; this at eight, and those about 20 feet broad. The present town of Circleville covers all the round and the western half of the square fort. These fortifications, where the town stands, will entirely disappear in a few years; and I have used the only means within my power, to perpetuate their memory, by the annexed drawing and this brief description.

Where the wall of the square fort has been manufactured into brick, the workmen found some ashes, calcined stones, sticks, and a little vegetable mould, all of which must have been taken up from the surface of the surrounding plain. As the square fort is a *perfect* square, so the gateways or openings are at equal distances from each other, and on a right line parallel with the wall. The walls of this work vary a few degrees from north and south, east and west; but not more than the needle varies, and not a few surveyors have, from this circumstance, been impressed with the belief that the authors of these works were acquainted with astronomy.— What surprized me, on measuring these forts, was the exact manner in which they had laid down their circle and square; so that after every effort, by the most careful survey, to detect some errour in their measurement, we found that it was impossible, and that the measurement was much more correct, than it would have been, in all probability, had the present inhabitants undertaken to construct such a work. Let those consider this circumstance, who affect to believe these antiquities were raised by the ancestors of the present race of Indians. Having learned something of astronomy, what nation, living as our Indians have, in the open air, with the heavenly bodies in full view, could have forgotten such knowledge?

Some hasty travellers, who have spent an hour or two here, have concluded that the "forts" at Circleville were not raised for military, but for religious purposes, because there were two extraordinary tumuli here. A gentleman in one of our Atlantick cities, who has never crossed the Alleghanies, has written to me, that *he* is fully convinced that they were raised for religious purposes. Men thus situated, and with no correct means of judging, will hardly be convinced by any thing I can say. Nor do I address myself to them, directly or indirectly; for it has long been my maxim, that it is worse than in vain to spend one's time in endeavouring to reason men out of opinions for which they never had any reasons.

The round fort was picketed in, if we are to judge from the appearance of the ground on and about the walls. Half way up the outside of the inner wall, is a place distinctly to be seen, where a row of *pickets* once stood, and where it was placed when this work of defence was originally erected. Finally, this work about its wall and ditch, eight years since, presented as much of a defensive aspect as forts which were occupied in our wars with the French, in 1755, such as Oswego, Fort Stanwix, and others. These works have been examined by the first military men now living in the United States, and they have uniformly declared their opinion to be, that they were military works of defence.

Ancient Works *on the* Main Branch *of* PAINT CREEK, Ohio.

The nearest of these are situated about eleven, and the furthest fifteen miles, westwardly, from the town of Chillicothe. The plate will assist us in describing them; to which we refer. Their contents, in acres and tenths, are set down on the plate. These works were very carefully surveyed by Mr. Perrin Kent, and the drawing was made by George Wolfley, Esq. of Circleville.

We shall begin with work *B*. situated on the farms of Capt. George Yocan, and Mr. John Harness. The gateways, it will be seen, are numerous, and are from eight to twenty feet wide. The walls are generally about ten feet high at this time, and rise to that height immediately at the gateways. These walls are composed of the common soil, which seems to have been taken up from no particular spot, but uniformly from near the surface. That part of this work which is square, has eight gateways; the sides of this square are sixty-six rods in length, containing an area of 27 acres 2 tenths. This part of the work has three gateways, connecting it with the larger one; one of which, is between two parallel walls, about four feet high. A small rivulet, rising towards the southwest side of the larger part of the largest work, runs through the wall, and sinks into the earth at *w. s.* Some suppose this sink hole to have been a work of art, originally. It is fifteen feet deep, and thirtynine across it, at the surface. There are two mounds, the one within, and another just outside of this work, represented by *m*, *m;* the latter is twenty feet high at this time.

Works at *A.* are all connected as represented in the plate. Their several contents will be seen by referring to it. The square work, it will be seen, contains exactly the same area with the square one be-

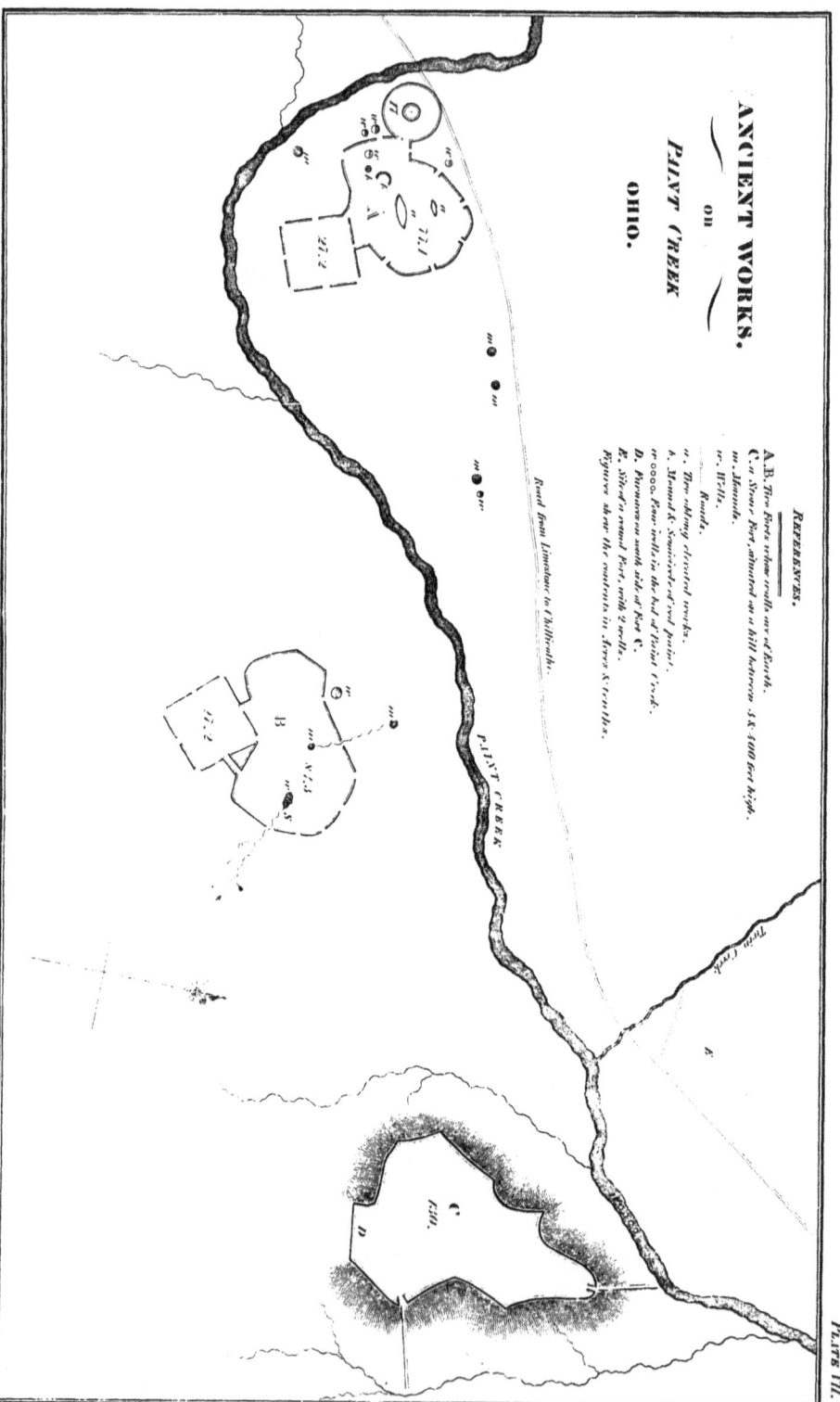

longing to *B.* and is, in all other respects, so much like that work, that to describe this, would be to repeat what has been said concerning the former. Such coincidences are very common, in our ancient works; so that a correct description of one, applies to hundreds in different parts of the country.

There is no mound within its walls, but there is one about ten feet high, nearly one hundred rods to the west of it. The large irregular part of the larger work, contains, as will be seen, 77.1 acres, in the walls of which are eight gateways, besides the two leading into the square just described. These gateways are from one to six rods in width, differing in that respect, very much one from another.

Connected by a gateway with this large work, is another in the northwest, sixty poles in diameter. In its centre is another circle, whose walls are now about four feet high, and this lesser circle six rods in diameter. There are three ancient wells at *w, w, w.* one of which is on the inside, the others on the outside of the wall. As the drawing shows, within the large work of irregular form, are two elevations, which are elliptical. The largest one is near the centre; its elevation is twentyfive feet; its longest diameter is twenty rods; its shortest, ten rods; its area is nearly one hundred and fiftynine square rods. This work is composed mostly of stones, in their natural state. They must have been brought from the bed of the creek, or from the hill. This elevated work is full of human bones. Some have not hesitated to express a belief, that on this work human beings were once sacrificed.

The other elliptical work has two stages; one end of it is only about eight feet high, the other end is fifteen. The surfaces of both are smooth. Such works are not as common here as on the Missisippi, and they are more common still further south, in Mexico.

There is a work in form of a half moon, set round the edges with stones, such as are now found about one mile from the spot from whence they were probably brought. Near this semicircular work, is a very singular mound, five feet high, thirty feet in diameter, and composed entirely of a red ochre, which answers very well as a paint. An abundance of this ochre is found on a hill not a great distance from this place; and from this circumstance, the name of the fine stream in the vicinity, in all probability is derived. It is called "Paint Creek."

The wells already mentioned, may be thus described. They are very broad at the top, one of them is six rods, another four; the former is now fifteen feet in depth, the latter ten. There is water in them, and they are like the one at Marietta, described by Dr. Hildreth. Near the limestone road, are several such ones.

The most interesting work, represented on the plate by C. remains to be noticed. It is situated on a high hill, believed to be more than three hundred feet in height, which is in many places almost perpendicular. The walls of this, consist of stones in their natural state. This wall was built upon the very brow of this hill, almost all around, except at *D.* where the ground is level. It had originally two gateways, at the only places where roads could be made to the interval below. At the northern gateway, stones enough now lie, to have built two considerable round towers. From thence to the creek is a natural, perhaps there was once an artificial, road. The stones lie scattered about in confusion, and consist mostly of what Mc. Clure would call the old red sand stone, taken from the sides of the hill on which this "walled town" once stood. Enough of these stones lie here, to have furnished materials for a wall four feet in thickness, and ten feet in height. On the inside of the wall, at line *D.* there appears to have been a row of furnaces or smiths' shops, where the cinders now lie many feet in depth.

I am not able to say with certainty, what manufactures were carried on here, nor can I say whether brick or iron tools were made here, or both. It was clay, that was exposed to the action of fire; the remains are four or five feet in depth, even now, at some places. Iron ore, in this country, is sometimes found in such clay; brick and potters' ware are manufactured out of it, in some other instances. This wall encloses an area of one hundred and thirty acres. It was one of the strongest places in this state, from its situation, so high is its elevation, so nearly perpendicular are the sides of the hill on which it stood.

The courses of the wall correspond with those of the very brow of the hill; and the quantity of stones is the greatest on each side of the gateways, and at any turn in the course of the wall, as if towers and battlements had been here erected. If the works at *A.* and *B.* were " sacred enclosures," this was the strong military work which defended them. No military man could have selected a better position for a place of protection to his countrymen, their temples, their altars, and gods.

In the bed of Paint Creek, which washes the foot of the hill on which the " walled town" stood, are four wells, worthy of our notice. They were dug through a pyritous slate rock, which is very rich in iron ore. When first discovered, by a person passing over them in a canoe, they were covered over, each, by a stone, of about the size, and very much in the shape, of the common millstone, now in use in our grist mills. These covers had a hole through their centre, through which a large pry or handspike might be put, for the purpose of removing them off and on the wells. The hole through the centre was about four inches in diameter. The wells at the top, were more than three feet in diameter, and stones well wrought with tools, so as to make good joints, as a stone mason would say, were laid around the several wells.

I had a good opportunity to examine these wells, the stream in which they are sunk, being very low. The covers are now broken to pieces, and the wells filled with pebbles. That they are works of art, is beyond a doubt. For what purpose they were dug, has been a question among those who have visited them, as the wells themselves are in the stream. The bed of the creek was not here in all probability, when these were sunk. These wells, with stones at their mouths, resemble those described to us in the patriarchal ages. Were they not dug in those days?

At *E.* is a circular work, containing between seven and eight acres, whose walls are not now more than ten feet high, surrounded with a ditch, except at one place, perhaps four rods broad, where there is an opening much resembling a modern turnpike road, leading down into the interval land, adjoining the creek. At the end of the ditch, adjoining the wall on each side of this road, is a spring of very good water. Down to the largest one is the appearance of an ancient road. These springs were dug down considerably, or rather the earth where they now rise, by the hand of man.

General William Vance's dwelling house now occupies this gateway, and his orchard and fruit yard the area within this ancient, sacred enclosure.

Ancient Works *at* PORTSMOUTH, Ohio.

Descending the Scioto to its mouth, at Portsmouth, we find an ancient work, which I doubt not was a military one of defence, situated on the Kentucky shore, nearly opposite the town of Alexandria. The reader is referred to the accurate drawing of all the works near this place, taken on the spot, from actual examination and survey. The importance of this place, it seems was duly appreciated by the people, who in "olden time" resided here. To their attachment to this part of the country, as well as the great population which must have been here, are we indebted for the striking and numerous traces of a once flourishing settlement.

The annexed plate will enable the reader to form a very correct idea of these ancient remains.

On the Kentucky side of the Ohio, opposite the mouth of the Scioto river, is a large fort, with an elevated, large mound of earth near its southwestern outside angle, and parallel walls of earth, as represented by *p, p, p, p*. The eastern parallel walls have a gateway leading down a high steep bank of a river to the water. They are about ten rods asunder, and from four to six feet in height at this time, and connected with the fort by a gateway. Two small rivulets have worn themselves channels quite through these walls, from ten to twenty feet in depth, since they were deserted, from which their antiquity may be inferred.

The fort is represented by *F.* on the plate, which is nearly a square, with five gateways, whose walls of earth are now from fourteen to twenty feet in height.

From the gateway, at the northwest corner of this fort, commenced two parallel walls of earth, extending nearly to the Ohio, in a bend of that river, where, in some low ground near the bank, they disappear. The river seems to have moved its bed a little, since these walls were thrown up. A large elevated mound at the southwest corner of the fort, on the outside of the fortification, is represented by *m*. It appears not to have been used as a place of sepulture; it is too large to have belonged to that class of Antiquities. It is a large work, raised perhaps twenty feet or more, very level on its surface, and I

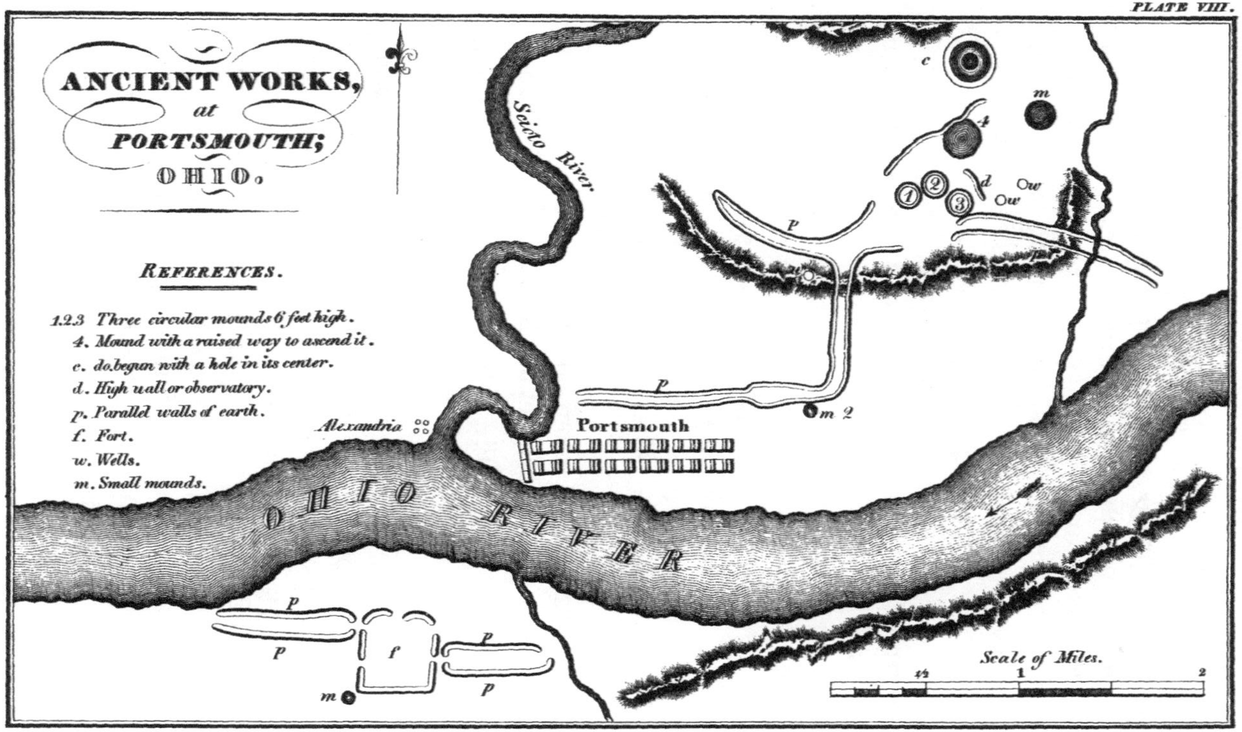

ANCIENT WORKS, at PORTSMOUTH; OHIO.

REFERENCES.

1.2.3 Three circular mounds 6 feet high.
4. Mound with a raised way to ascend it.
c. do. begun with a hole in its center.
d. High wall or observatory.
p. Parallel walls of earth.
f. Fort.
w. Wells.
m. Small mounds.

Scale of Miles.

Engraved for the American Antiquarian Society

PLATE VIII.

should suppose contains half an acre of ground. It seems to me, to have been designed for uses similar to the elevated squares at Marietta. Between these works and the Ohio, is a body of fine interval land, which was nearly enclosed by them, aided by the river, and a creek, which has high perpendicular banks. Buried in the walls of this fort, have been found and taken out, large quantities of iron, manufactured into pickaxes, shovels, gun barrels, &c. evidently secreted there by the French, when they fled from the victorious and combined forces of England and America, at the time fort Du Quesne, afterwards fort Pitt, was taken from them. Excavations made in quest of these hidden treasures, are to be seen on these walls, and in many other places near them.

Several of their graves have been opened and articles found, which leave no doubt on my mind as to their authors, nor any great doubt as to the time when they were deposited here.

On the north side of the river, are works still more extensive than these, more intricate, and of course, more impressive. We must again refer to the plate, in order to shorten our labour in description, and at the same time, give a clearer idea of them than otherwise could be obtained.

Commencing in the low ground, near the present bank of the Scioto river, which seems to have changed a little since these works were raised, are two parallel walls of earth, quite similar to those already described on the other side of the Ohio, as to their height, and their being composed of earth taken up uniformly from the surface, so as not to leave any traces by which we perceive from whence it was taken. This was probably owing to the rudeness of the tools used in constructing these walls. From the bank of the Scioto, they lead eastwardly, for a considerable distance, [as a reference to the scale on which these ruins are laid down will show, and which is an inch to a mile,] continuing about eight or ten rods apart, when, suddenly, they widen at a short distance to the east of the dwelling house of John Brown, Esq. and continue about twenty rods apart, with a curve towards the elevated ground, which they ascend in the manner represented by the drawing. This hill is very steep, and forty or fifty feet high; after rising which, we again find level land, and a fine rich, but ancient alluvion of the Ohio. Here, near a curve in the parallel walls, is a well on the brow of the hill, at this time twentyfive feet, perhaps, in depth; but from the immense quantity of rounded pebbles and sand, of which the earth here consists, after passing through the deep black vegetable mould on the surface, we are involuntarily led to believe, that this well was once quite deep enough to have its bottom on a level with the surface of the river, even in a low time of water in that stream.

The figures 1, 2, 3, represent three circular tumuli, elevated about six feet above the adjacent plain, and each of them contains nearly an acre. Not far from these, at 4, is a still higher similar work, so high, indeed, that it was necessary to throw up a way similar to a modern turnpike road, in order to ascend it. This work is now more than twenty feet in perpendicular height, and contains nearly one acre of ground. This elevated circular work, with raised walks to ascend and descend to and from its elevated area, was not used as a cemetery. Not far from it, however, there is one, near *m*, which is a conical mound of earth, brought to a point at its apex, at least twentyfive feet high, filled with the mouldering ashes of the people who constructed these works. In a northwestern direction is a similar one, just begun. It is surrounded by a ditch about six feet deep, with a hole in the centre of this circular work, which is represented by *c*. Two other wells, o, o, are now ten or twelve feet in depth, and appear to me to have been dug for water, and are similar to the one already described. Near these, at *d*, is a wall of earth, raised so high, that a spectator standing on its summit, may have a full view of whatever is transacting on the works 1, 2, 3, 4. This last work is easily ascended at each end.

From these extensive works on this " High Place," are two parallel walls of earth, leading to the margin of the Ohio, which are about two miles in length. They are from six to ten feet high. They are lost in the low ground near the river, which appears to have moved from them since they were constructed. Between these walls and the Ohio, is as fine a body of interval land as any along the valley of this beautiful stream; quite sufficient, if well cultivated, to support a considerable population. The surface of the earth, between all the parallel walls, is quite smooth, and appears to have been made so by art, and was used as a road, by those coming down either of the rivers, for the purpose of ascending to the " High Place," situated upon the hill. The walls might have served as fences also, to enclose the interval, which was probably cultivated.

On the low land I saw but one mound, *m.* 2. and that is a cemetery, but is not very large, and it appears to have belonged to the common people, probably those who resided near it on the plain.

Ancient Works *on the* LITTLE MIAMI RIVER.

These works have been much noticed by those who have travelled on the road which crosses them; and several partial accounts of them have already been published. But as some farther notice of these extraordinary remains of Antiquity may be here expected, the accompanying drawing and description are given.

Explanation *of the* Plate.

The fortification stands on a plain, nearly horizontal, about 236 feet above the level of the river, between two branches with very steep and deep banks. The openings in the walls are the gateways. The plain extends eastward along the state road, nearly level, about half a mile. The fortification on all sides, except on the east and west where the road runs, is surrounded with precipices nearly in the shape of the wall. The wall on the inside varies in its height, according to the shape of the ground on

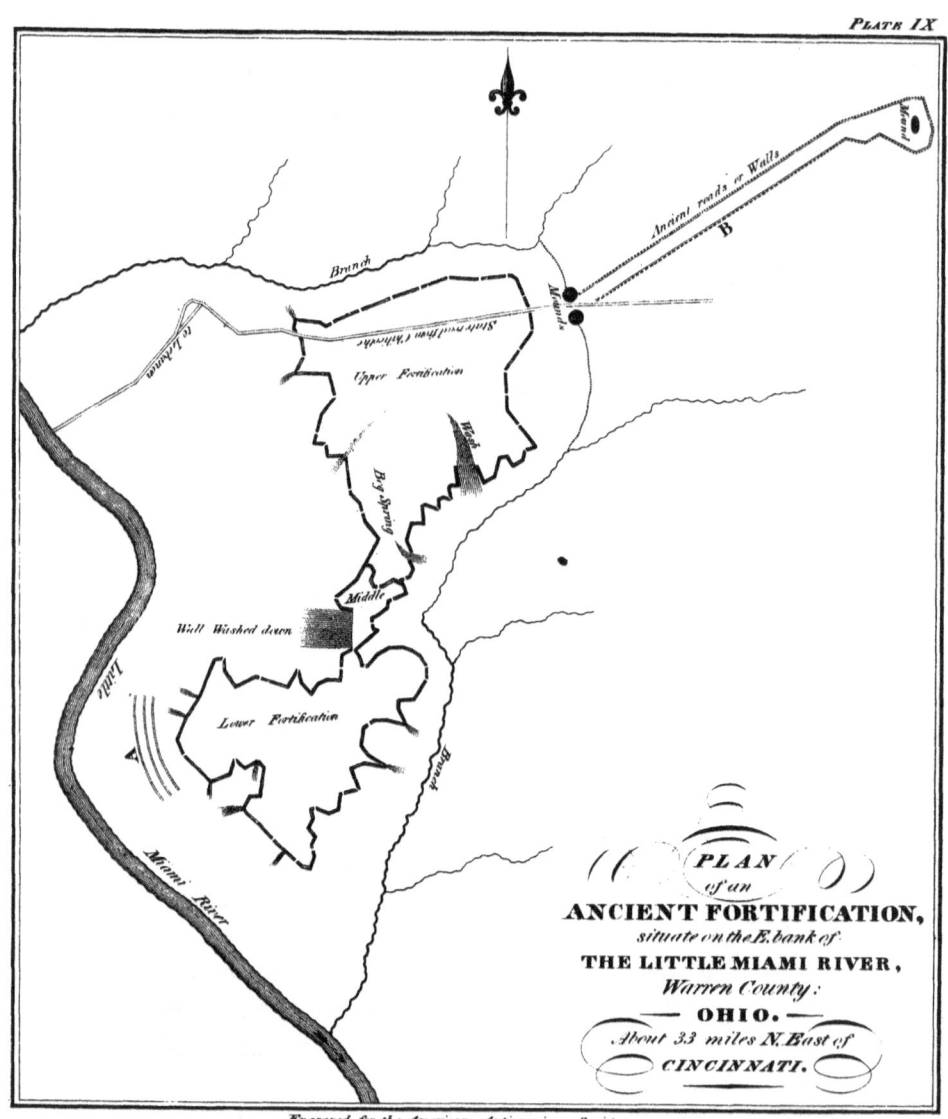

the outside, being generally from eight to ten feet. But on the plain it is about nineteen and an half feet high inside and out, on a base of four and a half poles. In a few places it appears to be washed away in gutters, made by water collecting on the inside.

At about twenty poles east from the gate, through which the state road runs, are two mounds, about ten feet eight inches high, the road running between them nearly equidistant from each. From these mounds are gutters running nearly north and south, that appear to be artificial, and made to communicate with the branches on each side. Northeast from the mounds, on the plain, are two roads, *B.* each about one pole wide, elevated about three feet, and which run nearly parallel, about one fourth of a mile, and then form an irregular semicircle round a small mound. Near the southwest end of the fortification are three circular roads, *A.* between thirty and forty poles in length, cut out of the precipice between the wall and the river. The wall is made of earth.

Many conjectures have been made as to the design of the authors in erecting a work with no less than 58 gateways. Several of these openings have evidently been occasioned by the water, which had been collected on the inside until it overflowed the walls, and wore itself a passage. In several other places the walls might never have been completed.

Some have supposed the whole was intended as a work of mere sport in the authors. I have always doubted whether any people of sane minds, would have ever performed quite so much labour in mere sport. Probably those openings were neither gateways, nor produced by the action of water, but were from some cause left unfinished.

Some persons, from the shape of these works, have even believed that the authors intended to represent by them the continents of North and South America! But the walls follow exactly the brow of the hill, and the works are built to suit the position of the ground, where it is hilly and precipitous; where it is not so, the walls suddenly rise to a far greater height.

The three parallel roads, *A*. dug at a great expense of labour, into the rocks and rocky soil adjacent and parallel to the Little Miami river, appear to have been designed for persons to stand on, who wished to annoy those who were passing up and down the river. The Indians, as I have been informed, made this use of these roads in their wars with each other and with the whites. Whether these works *all* belong to the same era and the same people, I cannot say, though the general opinion is, that they do. On the whole, I have ventured to class them among "Ancient Fortifications," to which they appear to have higher claims than almost any other, for reasons too apparent to require a recital.

The two parallel lines, *B*. are two roads very similar to modern turnpikes, and are made to suit the nature of the soil and make of the ground. If the roads were for foot races, the mounds were the goals from whence the pedestrians started, or around which they ran. The area which these parallel walls enclose, smoothed by art, might have been the place where games were celebrated. We cannot say that these works were designed for such purposes; but we can say, that similar works were thus used among the early inhabitants of Greece and Rome.

Speaking of the works of Antiquity found in the Miami country, Dr. Daniel Drake, an officer of the American Antiquarian Society, in his "Picture of Cincinnati," says, "of excavations we have but one," that is, belonging to the works of that place. "Its depth is about twelve feet. Its diameter, from the top of the circular bank, formed by throwing out the earth, is nearly fifty feet. It has the appearance of a half filled well; but no examination has yet been undertaken."

Dr. Drake proceeds to describe the ancient works where Cincinnati now stands. "The mounds or pyramids found on this plain were four in number. The largest stands directly west of the central enclosure, at the distance of five hundred yards. Its present height is twentyseven feet; and about eight feet were cut off by Gen. Wayne, in 1794, to prepare it for a centinel. It is a regular ellipsis, whose diameters are to each other, nearly as two to one. That which is greatest in length runs seventeen degrees east of north. Its circumference at the base is four hundred and forty feet. The earth, for thirty or forty yards around it, is perceptibly lower than the other parts of the plain, and the stratum of loam is thinner; from which it appears to have been formed by scooping up the surface; which opinion is confirmed by its internal structure. It has been penetrated nearly to its centre, and found to consist of loam, gradually passing into soil, with rotten wood. The fruits of this examination were only a few scattered and decayed human bones, a branch of a deer's horn, and a piece of earthen ware containing muscle shells. At the distance of five hundred feet from this pyramid, in the direction of north 8° east, there is another about nine feet high, of a circular figure, and nearly flat on the top. This has been penetrated to the centre of its base, without affording any thing but some fragments of human skeletons, and a handful of copper beads which had been strung on a cord of lint. The mound at the intersection of Third and Main streets has attracted most attention, and is the only one that had any connexion with the lines which have been described. It was eight feet high, one hundred and twenty long, and sixty broad, of an oval figure, with its diameters lying nearly in the direction of the cardinal points. It has been almost obliterated by the graduation of Main street, and its construction is therefore well known. Whatever it contained was deposited at a small distance beneath the stratum of loam which is common to the town.— The first artificial layer was of gravel, considerably raised in the middle; the next, composed of large pebbles, was convex and of an uniform thickness; the last consisted of loam and soil. These strata were entire, and must have been formed after the deposits in the tumulus were completed. Of the articles taken from thence, many have been lost; but the following catalogue embraces the most worthy of notice.

1. Pieces of jasper, rock crystal, granite, and some other stones, cylindrical at the extremes, and

swelled in the middle, with an annular groove near one end.

2. A circular piece of canal coal with a large opening in the centre, as if for an axis, and a deep groove; the circumference, suitable for a hand. It has a number of small perforations disposed in four equidistant lines, which run from the circumference towards the centre.

3. A smaller article of the same shape, with eight lines of perforations; but composed of argillaceous earth, well polished.

4. A bone, ornamented with several carved lines, supposed to be hieroglyphical.

5. A sculptural representation of the head and beak of a rapacious bird, perhaps an eagle.

6. A mass of lead ore, (galena) lumps of which have been found in other tumuli.

7. A quantity of isinglass, (mica membranacea) plates of which have been discovered in, and about other mounds.

8. A small oval piece of sheet copper, with two perforations.

9. A larger oblong piece of the same metal, with longitudinal grooves and ridges.

These articles are described in the fourth and fifth volumes of the American Philosophical Transactions by Governour Sargent and Judge Turner; and were supposed by Professor Barton to have been designed in part for ornament, and in part for superstitious ceremonies. In addition to which, the author says, he has since discovered in the same mound,

10. A number of beads, or sections of small hollow cylinders, apparently of bone or shell.

11. The teeth of a carniverous animal, probably those of a bear.

12. Several large marine shells, belonging perhaps to the genus buccinum, cut in such a manner as to serve for domestick utensils, and nearly converted into a state of chalk.

13. Several copper articles, each consisting of two sets of circular concavo convex plates; the interiour one of each set connected with the other by a hollow axis, around which had been wound some lint; the whole encompassed by the bones of a man's hand. Several other articles resembling these have been found in other parts of the town. They all appear to consist of pure copper, covered with the green carbonate of that metal. After removing this incrustation of rust from two pieces, their specifick gravities were found to be 7. 545 and 7. 857. Their hardness is about that of the sheet copper of commerce. They are not engraven or embellished with characters of any kind.

14. Human bones. These were of different sizes; sometimes enclosed in rude stone coffins, but oftener lying blended with the earth; generally surrounded by a portion of ashes and charcoal.*"

In this whole tumulus, the author says, there were not discovered more than twenty or thirty skeletons.

The other ancient works mentioned by Dr. Drake, have not, to my knowledge, been actually

* Drake's Picture of Cincinnati, p. 204, &c.

surveyed. If they have been, I have not seen any diagram sketches of them; a few remarks, therefore, on this subject may suffice.

Few or none of them appear to me to have been forts, indeed I have never seen one on the Great Miami, which seemed to me to deserve that appellation. Their being situated on a hill is by no means a certain indication that they were forts, or that they were ever military works, when it is recollected that most, if not all, the places of religious worship in Greece, Rome, Judea, &c. were on high hills, and are denominated "High Places" among the Jews. I have seen several small mounds of earth in the Miami country, and some small works, but the people who raised such works on the waters of the larger rivers of this state were not numerous; and, comparatively speaking, these works are few in number and small in size. Their authors seem to have preferred the beautiful plains and fertile hills of the slow winding Scioto, to the low marshy interval of the Miami. Those who wish for further remarks on the few works situated in the Miami country, are referred to Dr. Drake's "*Picture of Cincinnati.*" He seems to think that the traces of ancient works on the interval lands in the Miami country, are where these people had towns, which appears to me highly probable. These traces of ancient settlement being few, we may conclude that their authors were also few.

ANCIENT TUMULI.

There is another species of ancient works in this country which deserves our notice. They are conical mounds, either of earth or stones, which were intended for many sacred and important purposes. In many parts of the world similar mounds were used as monuments, sepulchres, altars, and temples.

The accounts of these works, found in the scriptures, show that their origin must be sought for among the Antideluvians. That they are very ancient, were used as places of sepulture, publick resort and publick worship, is proved by all the writers of ancient times, both sacred and profane. Homer frequently mentions them. He particularly describes the tumulus of Tytyus and the spot where it was. In memory of the illustrious dead, a sepulchral mound of earth was raised over their remains; which from that time forward became an altar, whereon to offer sacrifices, and around which, to exhibit games of athletick exercise. These offerings and games were intended to propitiate their manes, to honour and perpetuate their memories.

Prudentius, a Roman bard, has told us, that there were in ancient Rome just as many temples of gods as there were sepulchres of heroes; implying that they were the *same*.* Need I mention the tomb of Anchises, which Virgil has described, with the offerings there presented, and the games there exhibited? The sanctity of Acropolis where Cecrops

---
* " Et tot templa Deum, quot in urba sepulchra,
Heroum numerare licit."   Prudentius, liber i.

was inhumed? The tomb of the father of Adonis, at Paphos, whereon a temple dedicated to Venus was erected? The grave of Cleomachus, whereon stood a temple dedicated to the worship of Apollo? Finally, I would ask the classical reader if the words translated TOMB and TEMPLE, are not used as synonymous, by the poets of Greece and Rome? Virgil, who wrote in the days of Augustus, speaks of these tumuli as being as ancient as they were sacred, even in his time. Who has forgotten those lines, the reading of which gave him so much pleasure in the days of his childhood?

———Tumulum antiquæ Cereris, sedamque sacratam,
Venimus———.   Æn. lib. ii. v. 742.

In the first ages of the world, reason teaches us to believe, that the government of mankind was patriarchal; and the scriptures inform us that it was so. In infancy and childhood we naturally look up to our parents for support and education. The debt of gratitude increases until the beloved object of our filial affection is no more. Then all the endearments, of which we were the objects, through all our helpless years, present themselves to our view, and we anxiously seek, by some monument, to perpetuate the memory of those to whose kind care we are so greatly indebted. By what better means, could such an object be effected by a people unacquainted with the use of letters? What more lasting monument of filial respect could have been raised by a people thus situated? How simple, and yet how sublime? and calculated to endure while the world itself shall continue, unless destroyed by the sacrilegious hand of man.

A conical tumulus was reared, games were instituted, and certain offerings presented on stated anniversaries. In later times, after warriours arose, and performed great and mighty deeds, the whole tribe or nation joined to raise on some high place, generally, a lofty tumulus. At first, sacrifices might have been, and probably were, offered on these tumuli, to the true God, as the great author and giver of life; but in later times they forgot Him, and worshipped the manes of the heroes they had buried there.

The conical *mounds* in Ohio are either of stones or of earth. The former, in other countries and in former ages, were intended as MONUMENTS, for the purpose of perpetuating the memory of some important event; or as ALTARS, whereon to offer sacrifices. The latter were used as cemeteries and as altars, whereon, in later times, temples were erected among the people of Greece and Rome. Their existence and uses may be learned, by consulting the ancient writers, both sacred and profane.

In the scriptures we are informed, that Jacob erected a pillar of stones in order to perpetuate the recollection of a remarkable dream which he had, where he reposed, when journeying to visit Laban. A pile of stones was raised on the spot, where many years afterwards he parted with his brother Esau. This mound was to be a limit, which neither of them should in future pass without being considered as a trespasser on the other. When the Israelites crossed the Jordan, the priests raised a pile of stones, which were brought from the bed of that river. The reasons are assigned by the several historians which the reader can see at his leisure.

Gilgal was a heap of stones, where the Israelites encamped the first night after they crossed the Jordan. If the reader will consult a correct map of Palestine, he will see that Shiloh, Bethel, Jerusalem, &c. where the Jews assembled at various periods of their history, for publick worship, were all of them situated upon high hills.

DESCRIPTION *of the* MOUNDS, *or* TUMULI, *of* EARTH.

They are of various altitudes and dimensions, some being only four or five feet in height, and ten or twelve feet in diameter at their base, whilst others, as we travel to the south, rise to the height of eighty and ninety feet, and cover many acres of ground.

They are generally, where completed, in the form of a cone. Those in the north part of Ohio are inferiour in size, and fewer in number, than those along the river. These mounds are believed to exist from the Rocky Mountains in the west, to the Alleghanies in the east; from the southern shore of lake Erie to the Mexican Gulph, and though few and small in the north, numerous and lofty in the south, yet exhibit proofs of a common origin.

I shall begin with the tumuli on the Muskingum, which are not very numerous, nor comparatively interesting, until we descend to Morgan county, where are some on the head waters of Jonathan's Creek, whose basis are formed of well burnt bricks, between four and five inches square.— There were found lying on the bricks charcoal, cinders, and pieces of calcined human bones.— Above them, the mound was composed of earth, showing that the dead had been burned in the manner of several eastern nations, and the mound raised afterwards.

Descending the Muskingum to its mouth, we arrive at the celebrated works at Marietta, already noticed, but not fully described. It is with great pleasure, that here I avail myself of a communication from Dr. S. P. Hildreth, of Marietta.

"Marietta, July 19, 1819.

" In removing the earth which composed an ancient mound in one of the streets of Marietta, on the margin of the plain, near the fortifications, several curious articles were discovered the latter part of June last. They appear to have been buried with the body of the person to whose memory this mound was erected.

" Lying immediately over, or on the forehead of the body, were found three large circular bosses, or ornaments for a sword belt, or a buckler; they are composed of copper, overlaid with a thick plate of silver. The fronts of them are slightly convex, with a depression, like a cup, in the centre, and measure two inches and a quarter across the face of each. On the back side, opposite the depressed portion, is a copper rivet or nail, around which are two separate plates, by which they were fastened to the leather. Two small pieces of the leather were found lying between the plates of one of the bosses;

they resemble the skin of an old mummy, and seem to have been preserved by the salts of the copper. The plates of copper are nearly reduced to an oxyde, or rust. The silver looks quite black, but is not much corroded, and on rubbing, it becomes quite brilliant. Two of these are yet entire; the third one is so much wasted, that it dropped in pieces on removing it from the earth. Around the rivet of one of them is a small quantity of flax or hemp, in a tolerable state of preservation. Near the side of the body was found a plate of silver which appears to have been the upper part of a sword scabbard; it is six inches in length and two inches in breadth, and weighs one ounce; it has no ornaments or figures, but has three longitudinal ridges, which probably correspond with edges, or ridges, of the sword; it seems to have been fastened to the scabbard by three or four rivets, the holes of which yet remain in the silver.

"Two or three broken pieces of a copper tube, were also found, filled with iron rust. These pieces, from their appearance, composed the lower end of the scabbard, near the point of the sword. No sign of the sword itself was discovered, except the appearance of rust above mentioned.

"Near the feet, was found a piece of copper, weighing three ounces. From its shape it appears to have been used as a plumb, or for an ornament, as near one of the ends is a circular crease, or groove, for tying a thread; it is round, two inches and a half in length, one inch in diameter at the centre, and half an inch at each end. It is composed of small pieces of native copper, pounded together; and in the cracks between the pieces, are stuck several pieces of silver; one nearly the size of a four penny piece, or half a dime. This copper ornament was covered with a coat of green rust, and is considerably corroded. A piece of red ochre, or paint, and a piece of iron ore, which has the appearance of having been partially vitrified, or melted, were also found. The ore is about the specifick gravity of pure iron.

"The body of the person here buried, was laid on the surface of the earth, with his face upwards, and his feet pointing to the northeast, and head to the southwest. From the appearance of several pieces of charcoal, and bits of partially burnt fossil coal, and the black colour of the earth, it would seem that the funeral obsequies had been celebrated by fire; and while the ashes were yet hot and smoking, a circle of thin flat stones had been laid around and over the body. The circular covering is about eight feet in diameter, and the stones yet look black, as if stained by fire and smoke. This circle of stones seems to have been the nucleus on which the mound was formed, as immediately over them is heaped the common earth of the adjacent plain, composed of a clayey sand and coarse gravel. This mound must originally have been about ten feet high, and thirty feet in diameter at its base. At the time of opening it, the height was six feet, and diameter between thirty and forty. It has every appearance of being as old as any in the neighbourhood, and was, at the first settlement of Marietta, covered with large trees, the remains of whose roots were yet apparent in digging away the earth. It also seems to have been made for this single personage, as the remains of one skeleton only were discovered. The bones were much decayed, and many of them crumbled to dust on exposure to the air. From the length of some of them, it is supposed the person was about six feet in height.

"Nothing unusual was discovered in their form, except that those of the skull were uncommonly thick. The situation of the mound on high ground, near the margin of the plain, and the porous quality of the earth, are admirably calculated to preserve any perishable substance from the certain decay which would attend it in many other situations. To these circumstances, is attributed the tolerable state of preservation in which several of the articles above described were found, after laying in the earth for several centuries. We say *centuries*, from the fact that trees were found growing on those ancient works, whose ages were ascertained to amount to between four and five hundred years each, by counting the concentrick circles in the stumps after the trees were cut down; and on the ground, besides them, were other trees in a state of decay, that appeared to have fallen from old age. Of what language, or of what nation were this mighty race, that once inhabited the territory watered by the Ohio, remains yet a mystery, too great for the most learned to unravel.

"But from what we see of their *works*, they must have had *some* acquaintance with the arts and sciences. They have left us *perfect* specimens of circles, squares, octagons, and parallel lines, on a grand and noble scale. And unless it can be proved that they had intercourse with Asia or Europe, we now see that they possessed the art of working in metals."

[The above described articles are in the possession of Doctor Hildreth, and can be seen by any one desirous of viewing them.]

[The drawings of some of the articles found in the mound at Marietta, Ohio, June 1, 1819, described by Dr. Hildreth, are on the opposite page.

Figure 1. Back view of the silver ornament for a sword scabbard.—2. Front view of the same.—3. Front view of an ornament for a belt; silver face.—4. Back view of the same; of copper.—5. A copper plumb or pendent, with bits of silver in the fissures.—6. A stone with seven holes, like a screw plate, fourteen inches long, finely polished and very hard; this last was found in a field, back of the great mound.]

To this account I have only to add, that I have carefully examined the articles above described, and the spot where they were found, and that the description is a correct one. The accompanying drawings, made by Dr. Hildreth, are also correct. This mound was opened under the direction of his Excellency R. J. Meigs, jr. who intends soon to open the large mound at the same place.

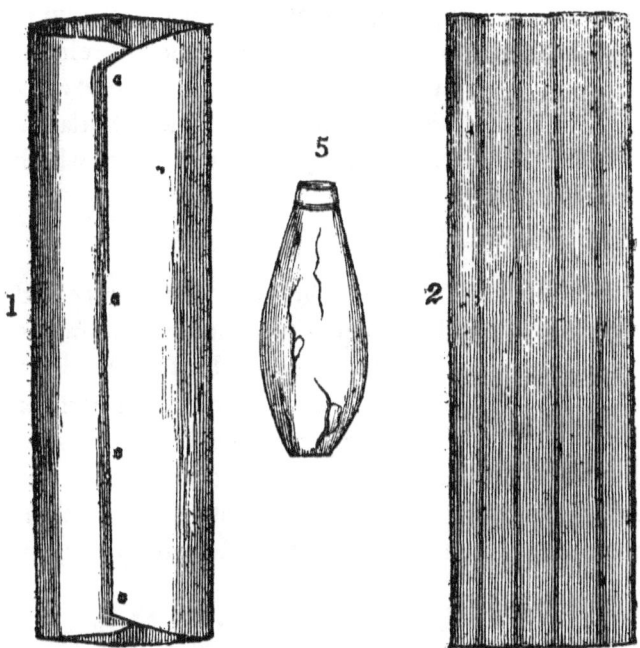

Figures 1, 2, 3 and 4, are a little less than two thirds as large; and 5 is two thirds as large, in length and breadth, as the articles they represent.

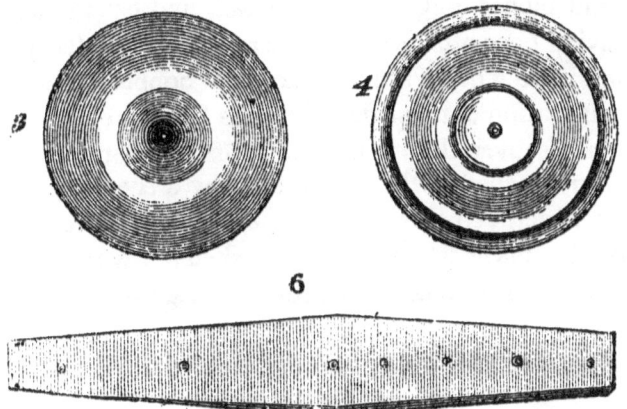

[Since the foregoing was written, a letter, giving some further information relating to ancient relicks, &c. has been received by the President of the American Antiquarian Society, from Dr. Hildreth, dated, "Marietta, 3d Nov. 1819," extracts from which are here inserted.]

"Dear Sir,

"Your favour of the 19th ultimo was received yesterday. I shall be happy to contribute all in my power towards promoting the objects of the Society, and will forward, by the first opportunity, a part, or all, of the curiosities in my possession, which were taken from an ancient mound in Marietta, the latter part of June last; of which I wrote a description, and which was published in the Marietta paper, in July.*

"In addition to the articles found at Marietta, I have procured, from a mound on the Little Muskingum, about four miles from Marietta, some pieces of copper, which appear to have been the front part of a helmet. It was originally about eight inches long and four broad, and has marks of having been attached to leather; it is much decayed, and is now quite a thin plate. A copper ornament in imitation of those described, as found in Marietta, was discovered with the plate, and appears to have been attached to the centre of it by a rivet, the hole for which remains both in the plate and ornament. At this place the remains of a skeleton were found. No part of it retained its form, but a portion of the

---

* This description is the same as that just given, which was communicated to C. Atwater, Esq.

forehead and skull, which lay under the plate of copper. These bones are deeply tinged with green, and appear to have been preserved by the salts of the copper.

"The mound in which these relicks were found, is about the magnitude of the one in Marietta, and has every appearance of being as ancient. I have in my possession some pieces of ancient potters' ware, found within the ancient works at Marietta. They are, some of them, neatly wrought, and composed of pounded flint stone and clay. They are yet quite solid and firm, although they have lain for several years, exposed to rain and frost, on the surface of the ground.

"We often find pieces of broken ware, near the banks of the river, and in the bottoms; but they are composed of clay and pounded clam shells; are much less compact and firm, and do not appear to have been burnt. They are evidently of the same composition with those made by the modern Indians.

"Some time in the course of this month, we propose opening several mounds in this place; and if any thing is discovered, which will throw light on the subject of the "*Ancients of the West,*" it shall be communicated to your Society, with a portion or all of the articles found. It seems to be a well established fact, that the bodies of nearly all those buried in mounds, were partially, if not entirely, consumed by fire, before the mounds were built. This is made to appear, by quantities of charcoal being found at the centre and base of the mounds; stones burned and blackened, and marks of fire on the metallick substances buried with them. It is a matter of much regret that on no one of the articles yet found, has been discovered any letters, characters, or hieroglyphicks, which would point to what nation or age these people belonged. I have been told by an eye witness, that a few years ago, near Blacksburgh in Virginia, eighty miles from Marietta, there was found about half of a *steel bow*, which, when entire, would measure five or six feet; the other part was corroded or broken. The father of the man who found it was a blacksmith, and worked up this curious article, I suppose, with as little remorse as he would an old gunbarrel. Mounds are very frequent in that neighbourhood, and many curious articles of Antiquity have been found there.

"I have also been told from good authority, that an ornament, composed of very pure *gold*, something similar to those found here, was discovered a few years since in Ross county, near Chillicothe, lying in the palm of a skeleton's hand, in a small mound. This curiosity, I am told, is in the Museum at Philadelphia."

The tumuli, in what is called the Scioto country, are both numerous and interesting. But south of lake Erie, until we arrive at Worthington, nine miles north of Columbus, they are few in number, and of small comparative magnitude. At the former place are some large ones; but I have made no survey of them, nor was it deemed important, as they so exactly resemble others which will be described.

Near Columbus the seat of government, were several mounds, one of which stood on an eminence in the principal street. It has been entirely removed, and converted into brick. It contained many human bones, some few articles, among which was an owl carved in stone, a rude, but very exact representation. In another part of the town was a tumulus of clay, which was also manufactured into bricks. In this were many human bones; but it was not, it would seem, their original place of deposit, as they lay in piles and in confusion.

As we still descend the Scioto, through a most fertile region of country, mounds and other ancient works frequently appear, until we arrive at Circleville, twentysix miles south of Columbus, where are to be seen some of the most interesting Antiquities any where to be found.

The works have been noticed, but the mounds remain to be described. Of these there were several which the ruthless hand of man is destroying. Near the centre of the round fort, a drawing of which is given in this work, was a tumulus of earth, about ten feet in height, and several rods in diameter at its base. On its eastern side, and extending six rods from it, was a semicircular pavement, composed of pebbles, such as are now found in the bed of the Scioto river, from whence they appear to have been brought.

The summit of this tumulus was nearly thirty feet in diameter, and there was a raised way to it, leading from the east, like a modern turnpike. The summit was level. The outline of the semicircular pavement and the walk is still discernible.— The earth composing this mound was entirely removed several years since. The writer was present at its removal, and carefully examined the contents. It contained,

1. Two human skeletons, lying on what had been the original surface of the earth.

2. A great quantity of arrow heads, some of which were so large, as to induce a belief that they were used for spear heads.

3. The handle either of a small sword or a large knife, made of an elk's horn; around the end where the blade had been inserted, was a ferule of silver, which, though black, was not much injured by time. Though the handle showed the hole where the blade had been inserted, yet no iron was found, but an oxyde remained of similar shape and size.

4. Charcoal and wood ashes, on which these articles lay, which were surrounded by several bricks very well burnt. The skeleton appeared to have been burned in a large and very hot fire, which had almost consumed the bones of the deceased. This skeleton was deposited a little to the south of the centre of the tumulus; and, about twenty feet to the north of it, was another, with which were

5. A large mirrour, about three feet in length, one foot and a half in breadth, and one inch and a half in thickness. This mirrour was of isinglass, (mica membranacea) and on it,

6. A plate of iron, which had become an oxyde; but before it was disturbed by the spade, resembled a plate of cast iron. The mirrour answered the purpose very well for which it was intended. This skeleton had also been burned like the former, and lay on charcoal and a considerable quantity of wood

ashes. A part of the mirrour is in my possession as well as a piece of a brick, taken from the spot at the time.

The knife, or sword handle, was sent to Mr. Peal's Museum, at Philadelphia.

To the southwest of this tumulus, about forty rods from it, is another, more than ninety feet in height, which is shown on the plate representing these works. It stands on a large hill, which appears to be artificial. This must have been the common cemetery, as it contains an immense number of human skeletons, of all sizes and ages.

The skeletons are laid horizontally, with their heads generally towards the centre, and the feet towards the outside of the tumulus. A considerable part of this work still stands uninjured, except by time. In it have been found, besides these skeletons, stone axes and knives, and several ornaments, with holes through them, by means of which, with a cord passing through these perforations, they could be worn by their owners.

On the south side of this tumulus, and not far from it, was a semicircular fosse, which, when I first saw it, was six feet deep. On opening it, was discovered at the bottom a great quantity of human bones, which, I am inclined to believe, were the remains of those who had been slain in some great and destructive battle. First, because they belonged to persons who had attained their full size; whereas, in the mound adjoining, were found the skeletons of persons of all ages; and secondly, they were here in the utmost confusion, as if buried in a hurry. May we not conjecture, that they belonged to the people who resided in the town, and who were victorious in the engagement? otherwise they would not have been thus honourably buried in the common cemetery.

The articles discovered in this mound, are of little value, though very numerous; something being found near the head of almost every individual.

In another mound, about a mile distant from this, was found a tool, almost exactly resembling one now in use among shoemakers, of which the following is a drawing, one half, each way, of the size of the utensil.

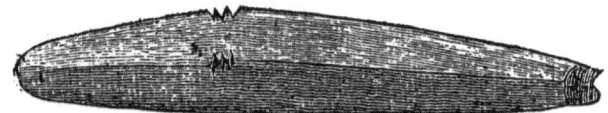

Descending the Scioto, mounds situated generally upon high hills, with a fair prospect towards the east, are frequently seen, until we arrive at Chillicothe, eighteen miles below Circleville.—Here, and in the immediate vicinity, were once several very interesting ones; but they are mostly demolished. Why were these wantonly destroyed? "They were rude." Were they not venerable on account of their high antiquity and simplicity? Are the modern Turks and Arabs, who trample on the busts of ancient heroes, the moss grown and prostrate columns of ancient temples, baths, palaces and theatres, the only barbarians? "But those who buried in tumuli, worshipped the manes of the heroes there deposited." And were not the Greeks and Romans also idolaters? And, have not all the civilized nations of Europe joined in condemning those who wantonly violate the sacred repositories of the dead, in those countries where the arts once flourished? It is true that the citizens of the ancient republicks enjoyed not the Christian religion; that commerce, and even agriculture, had made no great progress among them. To defend their country, and extend their conquests, were the great objects which they constantly kept in view. Soldiers became heroes; and these, after death, were exalted to gods. The love of military glory was constantly connected with the love of country. Having but few objects of pursuit, their passions were more intensely fixed on these. All nations but their own were considered as barbarians, and treated as such. They put to the sword, or sold as slaves, their prisoners of war. But what makes us to differ from them, unless it be an acquaintance with Christianity?

The Rev. Robert G. Wilson, D. D. of Chillicothe, a receiving officer of the American Antiquarian Society, has furnished me with authentick information concerning the mound, which once stood near the centre of the town. He took pains to write down every thing concerning its contents, at the time of its demolition. Its perpendicular height was about fifteen feet, and the diameter of its base about sixty. It was composed of sand, and contained human bones, belonging to skeletons which were buried in different parts of it. It was not until this pile of earth was removed, and the original surface exposed to view, that a probable conjecture of its original design could be formed. About twenty feet square of the surface had been levelled, and covered with bark. On the centre of this, lay a human skeleton, over which had been spread a mat, manufactured either from weeds or bark. On the breast lay what had been a piece of copper, in the form of a cross, which had now become verdigrise. On the breast also, lay a stone ornament with two perforations, one near each end, through which passed a string, by means of which it was suspended around the wearer's neck. On this string, which was made of sinews, and very much injured by time, were placed a great many beads, made of ivory or bone; for I cannot certainly say which. With these facts before us, we are left to conjecture at what time this individual lived; what were his heroick achievements in the field of battle; his wisdom and eloquence in the councils of his nation. But his cotemporaries have testified in a manner not to be mistaken, that among them, he was held in grateful remembrance.

The following is a correct drawing of the stone ornament, and saves me the trouble of a description of it. It is one half of the size of the stone in length and breadth.

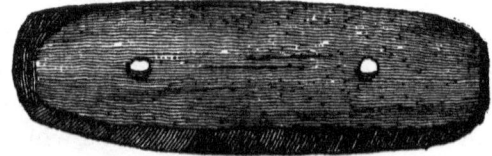

There are some very interesting works of Antiquity not far from Chillicothe, on the north fork of Paint Creek, a drawing of which is given in this volume.

ANCIENT WORKS,
on the
NORTH FORK OF PAINT CREEK
NEAR
CHILLICOTHE, OHIO.

Five miles and a half from Chillicothe, on the above mentioned stream, these works are situated on a beautiful piece of what we call second bottom. The area of the largest enclosure contains about one hundred and ten acres. On the northeast and west side of it, is a wall, with an intrenchment or ditch on its outside. It is generally twelve feet from the bottom to the summit of the wall, which is of earth. The ditch is about twenty feet wide, and the base of the wall the same. There is no ditch on the side next the river. The small work, on the east side, contains sixteen acres, and the walls are like those of the larger work, but there is no ditch. The largest circular work, which consists of a wall and ditch like those already described, is a sacred enclosure, including within it six mounds, which have been used as cemeteries. By examining the drawing and measuring them by the annexed scale, a correct idea of their dimensions may be easily obtained. The same observation applies to the gateways in the outer wall.*

The land on which these works are situated belongs to Mr. Ashley and Col. Evans, of Ross county.

The immense labour, and the numerous cemeteries filled with human bones, denote a vast population near this spot in ancient times.

* See the plan of the ancient works on the north fork of Paint Creek, opposite page 145.

Mounds *of* Stone.

Two such mounds have been described already in the county of Perry. Others have been found in various parts of the country. There is one, at least, in the vicinity of Licking river, not many miles from Newark. There is another on a branch of Hargus's Creek, a few miles to the northeast of Circleville. There were several not very far from the town of Chiliicothe.

If these mounds were sometimes used as cemeteries of distinguished persons, they were also used as monuments, with a view of perpetuating the recollection of some great transaction or event. In the former, not more, generally, than one or two skeletons are found; in the latter, none. These works are like those of earth, in form of a cone, composed of small stones, on which no marks of tools were visible. In them, some of the most interesting articles are found, such as urns, ornaments of copper, heads of spears, &c. of the same metal, as well as medals of copper, and pickaxes of hornblend; several drawings of which may be seen in this volume.

Works of this class, compared with those of earth, are few; and they are none of them as large as the mounds at Grave Creek, in the town of Circleville, which belong to the first class. I saw one of these stone tumuli which had been piled on the surface of the earth, on the spot where three skeletons had been buried in stone coffins, beneath the surface. It was situated on the western edge of the hill on which the "walled town" stood on Paint Creek. The graves appear to have been dug to about the depth of ours in the present times. After the bottoms and sides were lined with thin flat stones, the corpses were placed in these graves, in an eastern and western direction, and large flat stones were laid over the graves; then the earth, which had been dug out of the graves, was thrown over them. A huge pile of stones was placed over the whole. It is quite probable, however, that this was a work of our present race of Indians. Such graves are more common in Kentucky than Ohio.

No article, except the skeletons, was found in these graves; and the skeletons resembled, very much, the present race of Indians.

Mounds *beyond the Limits of the State of Ohio.*

These tumuli are very common on the river Ohio, from its utmost sources to its mouth. Few and small, comparatively, they are found on the waters of the Monongahela; but increase in number and size, as we descend towards the mouth of that stream, at Pittsburgh. Then rapidly increasing in number, they are of the largest dimensions at Grave Creek, below Wheeling. For an able and interesting account of those last mentioned, I am indebted to the Rev. Dr. Doddridge, of Brooke county, Virginia. An extract from his communication follows, dated,

"WELLSBURGH, VA. MAY 27, 1819.

"DEAR SIR,

"As to your inquiry concerning the ancient works at Grave Creek, below Wheeling, I will give you the best account which I can. Grave Creek flat is about eleven miles below Wheeling. It is about two miles square, consisting, for the most part, of second bottom, the most ancient alluvion; about the middle of it, little Grave Creek puts into the Ohio, and Great Grave creek, at the lower end of this flat. Between these creeks stand the ancient works, at the distance of about a quarter of a mile from the Ohio.

"The 'fortifications,' as they are called, are not remarkable ones, though a number of small mounds stand among them. In one of the tumuli, which was opened about twenty years since, sixty copper beads were found. Of these, I procured ten, and sent them to the Museum in Philadelphia. They were made of a coarse wire, which appeared to have been hammered out and not drawn, and were cut off at unequal lengths. They were soldered together in an awkward manner, the centre of some of them uniting with the edges of others. They were incrusted with verdigrise, but the inside of them was pure copper. This fact shows that the ancient inhabitants were not wholly unacquainted with the use of metals.

"The 'Big Grave,' as it is called, stands about half way between the two creeks, and about one fourth of a mile from the river. It is certainly one of the most august monuments of remote Antiquity any where to be found. Its circumference at the base, is three hundred yards; its diameter, of course, one hundred. Its altitude, from measurement, is ninety feet; and its diameter, at the summit, is forty-five feet. The centre, at the summit, appears to have sunk several feet,* so as to form a small kind of amphitheatre. The rim enclosing this amphitheatre, is seven or eight feet in thickness. On the south side, in its edge, stands a large beach tree, whose bark is marked with the initials of a great number of visitants.

"This lofty and venerable tumulus has been so far opened, as to ascertain that it contains many thousands of human skeletons, but no farther. The proprietor of the ground, Mr. Joseph Tomlinson, will not suffer its demolition in the smallest degree. I, for one, do him honour for his sacred regard for these works of Antiquity. I wish that the inhabitants of Chillicothe and Circleville had acted like Mr. Tomlinson. In that case, the mounds in those towns would have been left standing. They would have been religiously protected, as sacred relicks of remote and unknown Antiquity."

A careful survey of the above mentioned works, would probably show that they were all connected, and formed but parts of a whole, laid out with taste.

Following the river Ohio downwards, the mounds appear on both sides, erected uniformly on the highest alluvions along that stream. Those at Marietta, Portsmouth, and Cincinnati, are noticed else-

* Such a hollow place was always left in tumuli, until they were finished by bringing them to a perfect point.   C. A.

where. Their numbers increase all the way to the Missisippi, on which river they assume the largest size. Not having surveyed them, we shall use the description of Mr. Brackenridge, who has devoted great attention to them. With his discriminating powers of mind the publick are acquainted.

"These tumuli, as well as the fortifications, are to be found at the junction of all the rivers, along the Missisippi, in the most eligible positions for towns, and in the most extensive bodies of fertile land. Their number exceeds, perhaps, three thousand; the smallest not less than twenty feet in height, and one hundred in diameter at the base. Their great number, and the astonishing size of some of them, may be regarded as furnishing, with other circumstances, evidence of their antiquity. I have been sometimes induced to think, that, at the period when these were constructed, there was a population as numerous as that which once animated the borders of the Nile, or of the Euphrates, or of Mexico. The most numerous, as well as the most considerable of these remains, are found precisely in those parts of the country where the traces of a numerous population might be looked for, viz. from the mouth of the Ohio, on the east side of the river, to the Illinois river, and on the west side from the St. Francis to the Missouri. I am perfectly satisfied that cities, similar to those of ancient Mexico, of several hundred thousand souls, have existed in this country."

Nearly opposite St. Louis, there are traces of two such cities, in the distance of five miles. They are situated on the Cahokia, which crosses the American bottom opposite St. Louis. One of the mounds is eight hundred yards in circumference at the base, (the exact size of the pyramid of Asychis) and one hundred feet in height. Mr. Brackenridge, noticed "a mound at New Madrid of three hundred and fifty feet in diameter at the base." Other large ones are at the following places, viz. at St. Louis, one with two stages, another with three; at the mouth of the Missouri; at the mouth of Cahokia river, in two groups; twenty miles below, two groups also, but the mounds of a smaller size; on the bank of a lake, formerly the bed of the river, at the mouth of Marameck, St. Genevieve; one near Washington, Missisippi state, of one hundred and fortysix feet in height; at Baton Rouge, and on the bayou Manchac; one of the mounds near the lake is composed chiefly of shells. The inhabitants have taken away great quantities of them for lime.

The mound on Black River, has two stages and a group around. At each of the above places there are groups of mounds, and there was probably once a city. Mr. Brackenridge thinks that the largest city belonging to this people, was situated between the Ohio, Missisippi, Missouri, and Illinois. On the plains between the Arkansaw and St. Francis, there are several very large mounds.

Thus it will be seen, that these remains which were so few and small along the northern lakes, are more and more numerous as we travel in a southwestern direction, until we reach the Missisippi, where they are lofty and magnificent. Those works similar to the Teocalli of Mexico, by the Spaniards called "*Adoratorios*," are not found north of the mound at Circleville on the Scioto, or at least, I have seen none of them. They are very common and lofty, it seems, on the Missisippi river. An observing eye can easily mark, in these works, the progress of their authors, from the lakes to the valley of the Missisippi; thence to the Gulph of Mexico, and round it, through Texas, into New Mexico, and into South America; their increased numbers, as they proceeded, are evident; while the articles found in and near these works, show also the progressive improvement of the arts among those who erected them.

Should the patronage bestowed on this work, enable me to pursue my investigations, it is my intention to extend my survey quite down to the Mexican Gulph, and possibly beyond it; and if, through a want of patronage, a period should be put to my labours, yet, it is hoped, that others may be able to complete what, under untoward circumstances, I have begun.

Miscellaneous Remarks on the Uses of the Mounds.

Though they were used as places of sepulture and of worship, yet, Were they not sometimes, in the last resort, used also as places of defence? Solis, who describes the destruction of the Mexicans, and the conquest of their empire by the Spaniards, informs us that the "Teocalli," which were like many of our works, in cases of extreme necessity, appeared like "living hills;"* they were covered

* Brackenridge.

with warriours. Standing upon their altars and in their temples; upon the tombs of their fathers; defending themselves, their wives, their children, their aged parents, their country, and their gods, they fought with desperation. These mounds being elevated on high grounds, in situations easily defended, Is it not highly probable, that their authors, in cases of the last resort, used them as places of defence?

Some have expressed an opinion, that those which are situated within enclosures, were used as altars, whereon human victims were sacrificed.

Some, who have devoted great attention to our Antiquities, believe that the tumuli in front of the gateways of not a few of the works described, were placed there for idols, similar to the "Janitor gods" of Rome, to stand on. This proposition, which has some plausibility in it, we can neither assent to, nor deny, for want of sufficient data.

PLACES *of* DIVERSION.

By places of Diversion, we mean not those with which mounds are connected; the latter evidently were intended for the celebration of solemn games, instituted in honour of the dead.

The works we speak of under this head, are either round, like the small one, a short distance north of the square fort at Circleville, or they consist of two long parallel roads, resembling, in almost all respects, two turnpike roads. The circular ones, though frequently, nay generally, found in the vicinity of a great population in those days, consist of earth, raised but a few feet, by the aid of art, like a modern turnpike road, two rods or more in width, though sometimes less than one, being the highest in the centre, and gradually descending towards the outside. This road is perfectly smoothed by art. In the centre, the earth has a gentle and regular rise.

The oblong figure annexed,* is a representation of a great number of similar works, in various parts of this country. There are three such works between Circleville and Chillicothe, through which the present road passes.

If these works were not places of diversion, I cannot surmise for what purpose they were raised by their authors. They were of no use as places of defence. If intended for worship, or the celebration of games, near the tombs of their ancestors or chieftains, Why are they not connected with the mounds, instead of being uniformly placed at a distance from them? The number of such works, in various parts of the country, especially on the Scioto, Ohio, Kenhawa, Big Sandy rivers, &c. is considerable. They are so similar in structure, appearance, and situation, that the inference I draw from these circumstances is, that they were raised for similar purposes. Some persons have not failed to call them "roads;" but if so, Why are they always unconnected with other works? and, Why are they constructed either circular or in two long parallel lines, and these again connected at the ends?

* See the Plate.

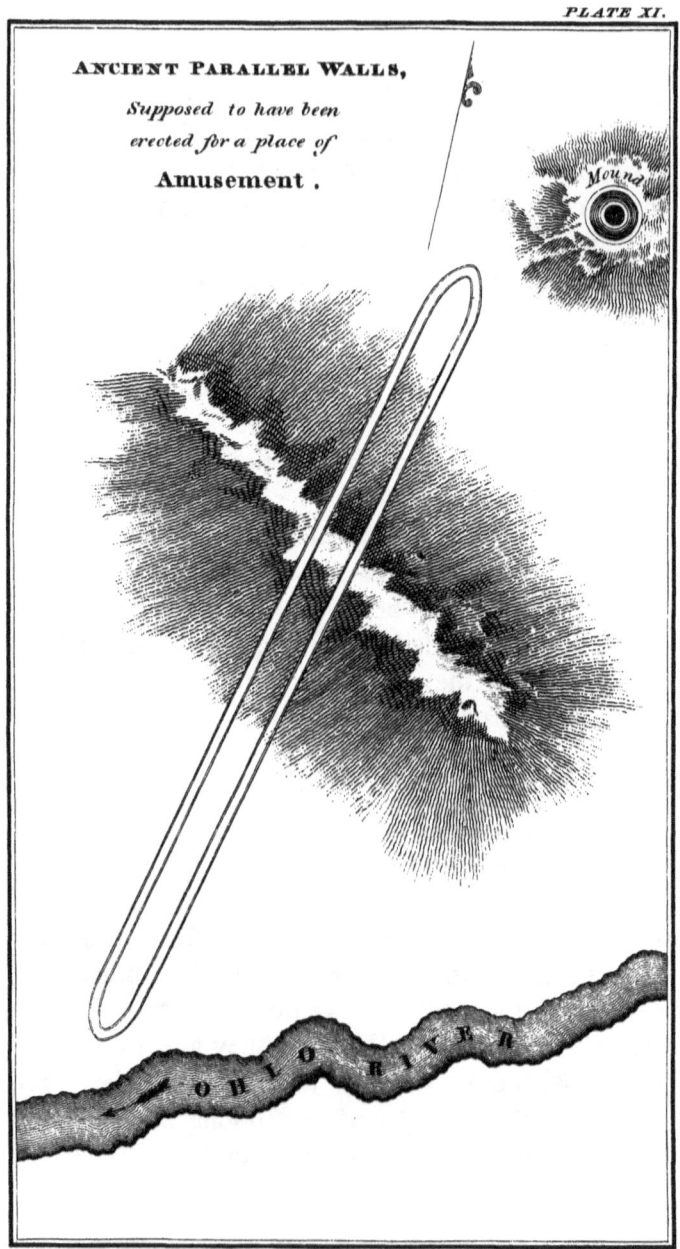

Parallel Walls of Earth.

Besides those above mentioned, there are parallel walls in most places, where other great works are found. Connected with the works on Licking Creek, are very extensive ones, as may be seen by referring to the plate which represents them. They were intended, I think, for purposes of defence, to protect persons who were travelling from one work to another. The two circular ones at Circleville were walls of the round fort. There are many others in various places, intended for similar purposes. But I am by no means sure, that all the walls of this description were intended as defensive; they might have been used as fences in some places, or as elevated and convenient positions, where spectators might have been seated, while some grand procession passed between them.

Near Piketon, on the Scioto, nineteen miles below Chillicothe, are two such parallel walls, which I did not measure, but can say without hesitation that they are now twenty feet high. The road leading down the river to Portsmouth, passes for a considerable distance between these walls. They are so high and so wide at their bases, that the traveller would not, without particular attention, suspect them to be artificial. I followed them the whole distance, and found that they lead in a direction towards three very high mounds, situated on a hill beyond them. It is easy to discover that these walls are artificial, if careful attention is bestowed on them.

Between these parallel walls, it is reasonable to suppose processions passed to the ancient place of sepulture; and what tends to confirm this opinion is, that the earth between them appears to have been levelled by art. On both sides of the Scioto, near these works, large intervales of rich land exist; and, from the number and size of the mounds on both sides of this stream, we may conclude that a great population once existed here.

Such walls as these are found in many places along the Ohio, but they generally lead to some lofty mounds situated on an eminence. Sometimes they encircle the mound or mounds, as will be seen by referring to some of the drawings in this volume; others are like those near Piketon. [*See the Plate.*]

CONJECTURES, *respecting the* ORIGIN *and* HISTORY *of the* AUTHORS *of the* ANCIENT WORKS *in* OHIO, &c.

The reader, after having become acquainted with many of our ancient works, naturally inquires, Who were their authors? Whence did they emigrate? At what time did they arrive? How long did they continue to inhabit this country? To what place did they emigrate? and, Where shall we look for their descendants?

These questions have often been asked, within the last thirty years, and as often answered, but not satisfactorily, especially to those who, on all occa-

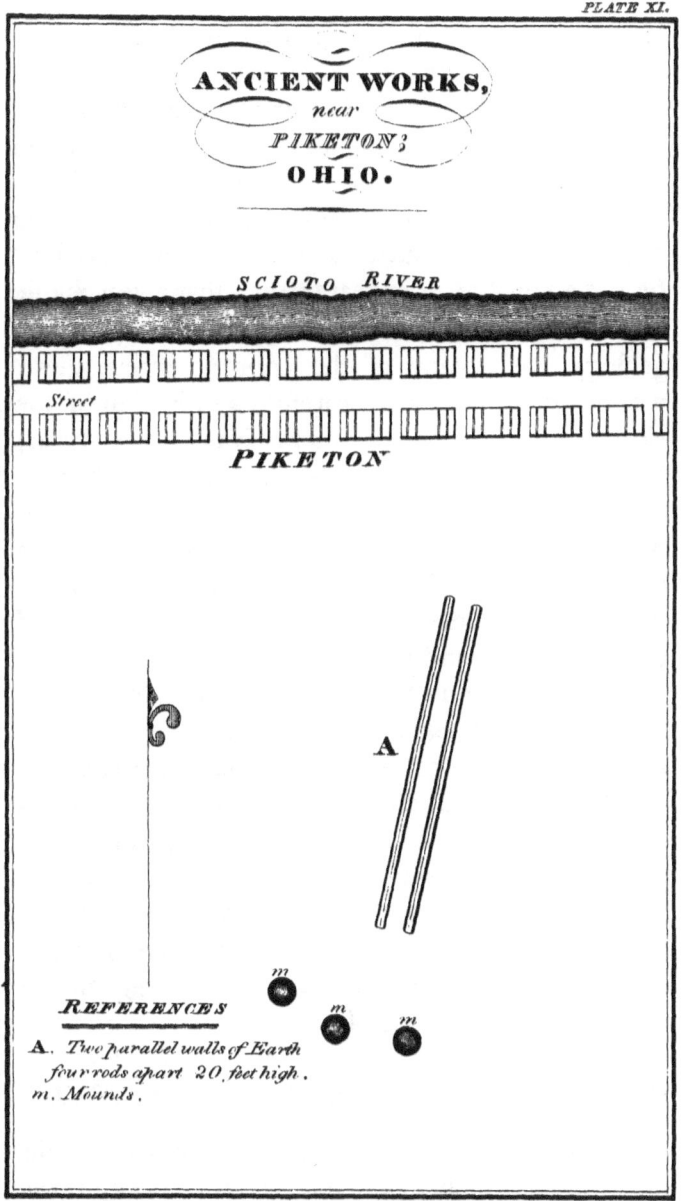

sions, require proofs amounting to mathematical certainty. Persons of this class, need not give themselves the useless labour of perusing the remaining part of this memoir. The nature of the subject does not admit of such proof, nor will the liberal and more enlightened portion of my readers require it at my hands. But if absolute certainty be not attainable, it appears to me that a reasonable one is—by obtaining a thorough knowledge of the geology and botany of the country where these works are found; by a careful examination of the skeletons of the people themselves; their dress; their ornaments, such as beads, bracelets, badges of office; their places of amusement, burial and worship; their buildings, and the materials used in their structure; their wells; domestick utensils; weapons of offence and defence; their medals and monuments, intended to perpetuate the memory of important events in their history; their idols; their modes of burial, and of worship; their fortifications, and the form, size, situation, and materials with which they were constructed. These are fragments of history, as Bacon would say, which have been saved from the deluge of time. Let us examine these fragments; let us also compare whatever belonged to this people in common with any other, either now or heretofore inhabiting this or any other part of our globe.

Who then were the Authors of our Ancient Works?

If we look into the Bible, the most authentick, the most ancient history of man, we shall there learn, that mankind, soon after the deluge, undertook to raise a tower high as heaven, which should serve to keep them together, as a place of worship, and stand to future ages as a monument of their industry, their religious zeal, their enterprize, their knowledge of the arts. Unacquainted, as they undoubtedly were, with the use of letters, in what better way could their names have been handed down to their posterity with renown? But in this attempt they were disappointed, and themselves dispersed through the wide world. Did they forget to raise afterwards, similar monuments and places of worship? They did not; and, to use the words of an inspired penman, "high places," of various altitudes and dimensions, were raised " on every high hill, and under every green tree," throughout the land of Palestine, and all the east.

Some of these " high places" belonged to single families, some to a mighty chieftain, a petty tribe, a city, or a whole nation. Some were places of worship for the individual, the tribe, the village, the town, the city, or the nation, to which they respectively belonged.

At those "high places," belonging to great nations, great national affairs were transacted. Here they crowned and deposed their kings; here they concluded peace and declared war. Here the nation assembled at stated seasons, to perform the solemn worship of their deities. Here they celebrated anniversaries of great national events, and buried the illustrious dead.

The Jews, on many great occasions, assembled at Gilgal. The name of the place, signifies "a heap."

Here was a pile of stones, which were brought from the bed of the river Jordan, and piled up on the spot where they encamped for the first night after they crossed that river, on their entrance into "the promised land." Let the reader examine similar piles of stones on the waters of the Licking, near Newark, in the counties of Perry, Pickaway and Ross, and then ask himself, Whether those who raised our monuments, were not originally from Asia? Shiloh, where the Jews frequently assembled to transact great national affairs, and perform acts of devotion, was situated upon a high hill. When this place was deserted, the loftier hill of Zion was selected in its stead. Upon Sinai's awful summit the law of God was promulgated. Moses was commanded to ascend a mountain to die. Solomon's temple was situated upon a high hill by Divine appointment. Samaria, a place celebrated for the worship of idols, was built upon the high hill of Shemer, by Omri, king of Israel, who was there buried. How many hundreds of mounds in this country are situated on the highest hills, surrounded by the most fertile soils? Traverse the counties of Licking, Franklin, Pickaway and Ross; examine the loftiest mounds, and compare them with those described as being in Palestine. Through the wide world, such places seem to have been preferred by the men of ancient times who erected them. In England, Scotland, and Wales, they are thus situated. For what we are about to quote concerning them, we are indebted to Pennant's Tour.*

* Vol. III. pages 66 and 67, fourth London edition, and refer to Plate VIII.

By examining Pennant's drawing and description of the Antiquities of Delvin, otherwise called Inch-Tuthel, on the river Tay, the reader will see how much the works on the Tay resemble ours on the Licking, near Newark. Pennant, however, imagines these to be Roman works, but Boethius, the only authority quoted by him, says, that Delvin is a work of the ancient Picts, and was by them called "Tulina." The reader is requested to compare the works near Newark, with those of Delvin.

The camp at Comerie, is also described by Pennant.* The learned author will have this a Roman work also; yet all the authorities quoted by him ascribe it to the Picts. The camp, as Pennant calls it, is on a water of Ruchel, situated on a high alluvion, like many of ours in the west. The Antiquities of Ardoch, also, the learned author will persist in ascribing to the Romans.† These works are on a water of Kneck. Without any authority whatever, Pennant ascribes them to Agricola.— Their walls, ditches, gateways, mounds of defence before them, and every thing about them, resemble our works here. The reader is invited to make the comparison. Pennant's imaginary Prætorium, is exactly like the circular works around our mounds, when placed within walls of earth. "Catter-thun,"‡ two miles from Angus, is ascribed by the learned tourist to the Caledonians, but such works are very common in Ohio. Such have been already described in this memoir.

* Vol. III. page 96.   † Ib. p. 102.   ‡ Ib. p. 158.

The same author describes two works on the river Loder or Lowthee, and one near the river Eimet,* exactly like ours in the west. The strong resemblance between the works in Scotland and ours, I think no man will deny.

I shall not trouble myself to examine authorities, as to works of the same kind in various parts of the British isles, because I might fatigue without instructing the reader. What has been said already, applies to many, very many others, throughout England, Scotland, Ireland and Wales. They were places of worship, burial, and defence, for the Picts, so called by the Romans, because they painted themselves, like the aborigines of this continent.

The acquaintance of the Egyptians with the useful and ornamental arts, was of an earlier date than that of the nations around them. Their pyramids and temples, medals and monuments, show us a comparatively civilized people, whilst their neighbours were rude barbarians—the former were shepherds, the latter hunters. In Egypt, a lofty pyramid is a place of sepulture and an altar, whilst a rude pile of stones at Gilgal, is raised for the purpose of commemorating a great national event.

The land of Ham, seems to have been the place where the arts were first nursed. A thickly crowded population, inhabiting a fertile soil, intersected by a large river, were placed in the most favourable circumstances for obtaining an acquaintance with the arts and sciences. The Nile fertilized their

* Vol. I. page 276, and plate 19, Nos. 1, 2 and 3.

fields, and wafted on its waves the bark of the mariner, while beneath its unruffled surface it contained an abundance of fishes. It invited to trade, to enterprize, and wealth. The people flourished and the arts were fostered. The same remarks apply to the people of the Indus and the Ganges—the results were similar. The banks of these streams were first cultivated. When other parts of the world were peopled, we have reason to believe, that it was done, either by fugitives from justice or from slavery. Their low origin will account for their low vices, and their ignorance. Living in countries but thinly settled, their improvement in their condition was gradual, though steady.

It is interesting to the philosopher, to observe the progressive improvements made by man in the several useful arts. Without letters, in the first rude stages of society, the tree is marked with a view to indicate what is already done, or is intended to be done. Though our Indians had lived along our Atlantick border for ages, yet they had advanced no farther in indicating projected designs, or in recording past events. The abundance of wild game, and the paucity of their numbers, will satisfactorily account for their ignorance in this, and almost every other respect. Coming here at an early age of the world, necessity had not civilized them. At that period, in almost all parts of the globe then inhabited, a small mound of earth served as a sepulchre and an altar, whereon the officiating priest could be seen by the surrounding worshippers.

For many ages we have reason to believe there were none but such altars. From Wales, they may be traced to Russia, quite across that empire, to our continent; across it from the mouth of the Columbia on the Pacifick ocean, to Black River, on the east end of lake Ontario. Thence turning in a southwestern direction, we find them extending quite to the southern parts of Mexico and Peru.

In the Russian empire, mounds are numerous, and were every where seen by the learned Adam Clarke, LL. D. in his tour from St. Petersburg to the Crimea, in the year 1800. In his travels in Russia, Tartary, and Turkey,* the author, in speaking of the country between St. Petersburg and Moscow, says, "Conical mounds of earth or tumuli occur very frequently. The most remarkable may be seen between Yezolbisky and Valdai, on both sides of the road, but chiefly on the left; and they continue to appear from the latter place to Jedrova. Professor Pallas has given a representation of four of those tumuli in a vignette at the beginning of his late work. They are common all over the Russian empire." Again,† the author says, "There are few finer prospects than that of Woronetz, viewed a few versts from the town on the road to Paulovsky. Throughout the whole of this country are seen dispersed over immense plains, mounds of earth, covered with a fine turf, the sepulchres of the ancient world, common to almost

* Vol. I. page 21, second Newyork edition.
† The same Vol. page 136.

every habitable country. If there exists any thing of former times, which may afford monuments of antediluvian manners, it is this mode of burial.— They seem to mark the progress of population in the first ages, after the dispersion, rising wherever the posterity of Noah came. Whether under the form of a mound in Scandinavia and Russia, a barrow in England, a *cairn* in Ireland, Scotland, and Wales, or those heaps, which the modern Greeks and Turks call *Tepe;* lastly, in the more artificial shape of a pyramid in Egypt; they had universally the same origin. They present the simplest and sublimest monuments, which any generation could raise over the bodies of their progenitors; calculated for almost endless duration, and speaking a language more impressive than the most studied epitaph upon Parian marble. When beheld in a distant evening's horizon, skirted by the rays of the setting sun, and touching, as it were, the clouds which hang over them, imagination pictures the spirits of heroes of remoter periods descending to irradiate the warriour's grave. Some of them rose in such regular forms, with so simple and yet so artificial a shape, in a plain, otherwise so perfectly level and flat, that no doubt whatever could be entertained respecting them. Others, still more ancient, have at last sunk into the earth, and left a hollow place, which still marks their pristine situation. Again, others, by the passage of the plough upon their surfaces, have been considerably diminished."

How exactly does this description of Clarke's apply to our mounds in the west? Who ever described with more accuracy, that species of mounds of earth in Ohio, which were used as cemeteries? Unless we knew to the contrary, who of us in Ohio, would ever suspect, that Dr. Clarke was not describing with fidelity, our western mounds? In one conjecture, however, he is mistaken; that is, in supposing those to be the most ancient, which were but just begun. I have seen them in all stages, from the time that a circular fosse, with a hole in its centre, was made, until these mounds were brought to a perfect point at the summit.

In Scioto county, a few miles from Portsmouth, is a circular fosse, with a hole in the centre of the area which it encloses. The owner makes use of this work as a barn yard.

There is a work of a similar form between two walls, belonging to the works at Newark; and I have seen several on the Kenhawa river, not far from Point Pleasant, and others, left in the same unfinished state, in a great number of places. It would seem that where a ditch was to enclose a tumulus, this ditch was first dug, then a hole made in the centre, which was covered over with wood, earth, stones, or brick, then a large funeral pile constructed, and the corpse of some distinguished personage placed on it and burnt. An examination of the works already described, will amply justify these conjectures.

I have a brick, now before me, over which lay, when found, wood ashes, charcoal, and human bones, burnt in a large and hot fire. And from what was found at Circleville, in the mound already described, it would seem that females were sometimes burnt with the males. I need not say, that this custom was derived from Asia, as it is well known to all my readers, that that is the only country to look to for the origin of such a custom.—The Greeks and Romans practised burning their illustrious dead. It was practised by several other nations, but they all derived it from Asia.

In the same volume of travels, * Dr. Clarke says, "Tumuli, so often mentioned before, abound in all steppes; and, in working the cliff for a magazine, or storehouse, where one of these tumuli had been raised, they found, in the sandy soil of which it consisted, an arched vault, shaped like an oven, constructed of large square bricks, and paved in a style of exquisite workmanship with the same materials."

We are told by the same author,† that "The Cossacks at Ekaterinedara, dug into some of these mounds for the purpose of making cellars, and found several ancient vases." Such vases are discovered in ours. Several have been found in our mounds, which resemble one found in Scotland, and described by Pennant. Another, somewhat resembling a small keg in its construction, and a tea kettle in the use to which it was put, is represented by the following drawing *(A.)* This vessel appears to be made of a composition of clay and shells.

*Vol. I. page 294.   † Clarke's Travels, Vol. I. p. 236.

Dr. Clarke informs us, that the bones of horses, as well as human bones, were found in some mounds in Russia. The teeth of bears, otters and beavers, are found in ours, lying beside the bones of human beings; but no bones of horses have been found to my knowledge.

Thus we learn from the most authentick sources, that these ancient works existing in Europe, Asia, and America, are as similar in their construction, in the materials with which they were raised, and in the articles found in them, as it is possible for them to be. Let those who are constantly seeking for some argument, with which to overthrow the history of man by Moses, consider this fact. Such persons have more than once asserted, that there were different stocks or races of men; but this similarity of works almost all over the world, indicates that all men sprung from one common origin.

I have always considered this fact, as strengthening the Mosaic account of man, and that the scriptures throw a strong and steady light on the path of the Antiquarian.

Another quotation from the learned, ingenious, and interesting Clarke, and we have done with him. In Tartary, he found a place called "Inverness," situated in the turn of a river. He inquired the meaning of the word, and found that "Inverness," in their language, signifies *in a turn.* Whoever looks into Pennant's Tour, will see a plate, representing a town, in the turn of a river in Scotland, called by the same name.

The names of not a few of the rivers in England, Scotland, and Wales, are the names also of rivers in Tartary. Will any one pretend that the inhabitants of Britain emigrated to Tartary, and carried the names of their towns and rivers along with them? The Danes, who descended from the Scythians, made settlements and conquests on the British isles, even since the days of Julius Cæsar.

The Scythians, from whom the Tartars are descended in all probability, first peopled the British isles. The fact, that our works are in all respects like those in Britain, and that similar works may be found all the way from this part of America to Tartary, furnishes no contemptible proof, that the Tartars were the authors of ours also. But were the ancestors of our North American Indians the authors of our works? Had not such an opinion been advanced by some great and good men in the

United States, the foundation on which it rests is so frail, that I certainly should not trouble myself or my readers to refute it. Never having particularly examined any of our ancient works, these writers contend that all of them were erected for purposes of defence—that the immense number of them proves that the ancestors of our Indians, having been engaged in continual civil wars, their numbers were so thinned and the remainder of them so scattered, that they lost the knowledge of those arts which they formerly possessed; and, from the shepherd state of society, reverted to that of the hunter.

First, then, as to the immense number of military works. They are not here. The lines of forts, if forts they were, commencing near Cataraugus Creek; those at Newark, at Circleville, on Paint Creek, one on the Miami, and one opposite Portsmouth, have been described. And I by no means believe that even all these were real forts. Between the Rocky Mountains and the Alleghanies, the northern Lakes and the Mexican Gulph, it may be possible, that there were originally about twenty forts, to defend a country nearly as large as Europe; and these were probably two thousand years in building, situated too in a thickly settled country! By assuming facts, existing only in the writer's imagination, how easily he can prove whatever he pleases. Thus falls the main pillar on which this opinion rested. They are not military works. But by being engaged in long and destructive wars, the ancestors of our present race of Indians lost the knowledge—of what? of constructing *military* works. I should have drawn from such premises a conclusion exactly the reverse of this. I should have supposed, that the longer any people were engaged in war, the greater, in the same ratio, would be their knowledge of the art of war. Placed in such a situation, in every other part of the world, man has rapidly improved in this art. To such circumstances, many inventions and improvements owe their origin. Was there no Archimedes in the west? or, Have not the people been slandered?

As to the number of their wars, I can say nothing, because there is no history of them; but as to the number of forts here, I say they are few, and justify no such inferences as have been attempted to be drawn.

Have our present race of Indians ever buried their dead in mounds? Have they constructed such works as are described in the preceding pages? Were they acquainted with the use of silver, or iron, or copper? All these, curiously wrought, were found in one mound at Marietta. Did the ancestors of our Indians burn the bodies of distinguished chiefs on funeral piles, and then raise a lofty tumulus over the urn which contained their ashes? Did the North American Indians erect any thing like the "walled town" on Paint Creek? Did they ever dig such wells as are found at Marietta, Portsmouth, and above all, such as those on Paint Creek? Did they manufacture vessels from calcareous breccia, equal to any now made in Italy? Did they ever make and worship an idol, representing the three principal gods of India? If any person can answer any one of these questions in the affirnative, let him state facts minutely; and let this be done, not by a mere traveller, whose credulity has been practised upon by either red or white men.

By referring to the works of those American writers who have affected to believe that *all* our Antiquities belonged to the ancestors of our North American Indians, it will be seen, that this opinion has been advanced to refute the representations of some Europeans, that our climate was debilitating in its effects upon the bodies and minds of the people of America, and that nature belittled every thing here. In answer to this false theory, Were our writers so hardly pressed for arguments, that they were obliged to resort to another theory equally unfounded in truth? Does not their argument prove exactly the reverse of what they contend for? Well might their opponents say to our writers, "It is true that all your ancient works in the west, were raised by the ancestors of your Indians in North America. When they came into your country they were half civilized, but such were the debilitating effects of your climate upon both their bodies and minds, that they degenerated into savages in the lowest state of barbarism." When proofs are brought forward that our climate or civil wars have produced such a deplorable effect, we may then believe it.

The skeletons found in our mounds never belonged to a people like our Indians. The latter are a tall, rather slender, strait limbed people; the former were short and thick. They were rarely over five feet high, and few indeed were six. Their foreheads were low, cheek bones rather high; their faces were very short and broad; their eyes were very large; and, they had broad chins. I have examined more than fifty skulls found in tumuli, several of which I have before me. The drawing which I have given, is a fair specimen of them.— It is one eighth part of the size of the skull from which it was taken. *(C.)*

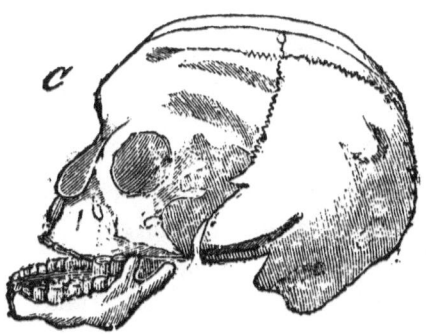

The limbs of our fossils are short and very thick, and resemble the Germans, more than any Europeans with whom I am acquainted.

An idol found in a tumulus near Nashville, Tennessee, and now in the museum of Mr. Clifford, of Lexington, Kentucky, will probably assist us in forming some idea, as to the origin of the authors of our western Antiquities. Like the "Triune vessel," hereafter mentioned, it was made of a clay peculiar for its fineness and its use, which is quite abundant in some parts of Kentucky. With this clay, was mixed a small portion of gypsum, or sulphat of lime.

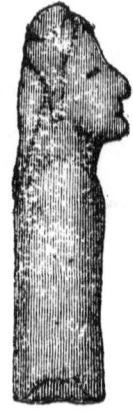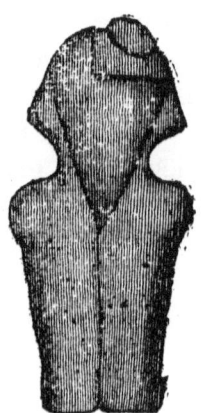

This idol* represents, in three views, a man in a state of nudity, whose arms have been cut off close to the body, and whose nose and chin have been mutilated; with a fillet and cake upon his head. In all these respects, as well as in the peculiar manner of plaiting the hair, it is exactly such an idol as Professor Pallas found in his travels in the southern part of the Russian empire.†

The idol discovered near Nashville, shows from whence its worshippers derived their origin and their religious rites. The "Triune idol or vessel," shows, in my opinion, that its authors originated in Hindostan, and the one now under consideration

---

* The original drawing of the three views of this idol was made by Miss Sarah Clifford, of Lexington, Kentucky, from which the above was taken.

† Pallas's Travels, Vol. II. Vignette No. II.

induces a belief, that some tribes were from countries adjacent.*

If the ancestors of our North American Indians were from the northern parts of Tartary, those who worshipped this idol came from a country lying farther to the south, where the population was dense, and where the arts had made great progress. While the Tartar of the north, was a hunter and a

---

*Those who wish to be acquainted with what the poets have said, concerning human sacrifices among the Greeks, may consult the Æneid, lib. II. v. 116.

 Sanguine placâstis ventos, et virgine cæsâ,
 Cum primùm Iliacas Danai venistis ad oras;
 Sanguine quærendi reditus, animâque litandum
 Argolicâ. Vulgi quæ vox ut venit ad aures,
 Obstupuere animi, gelidusque per ima cucurrit
 Ossa tremor; cui fata parent, quem poscat Apollo,
 Hìc Ithacus vatem magno Calchanta tumultu
 Protrahit in medios; quæ sint ea numina Divûm
 Flagitat; et mihi jam multi crudele canebant
 Artificis scelus, et taciti ventura videbant.
 Bis quinos silet ille dies, tectusque recusat
 Prodere voce suâ quenquam, aut opponere morti.
 Vix tandem magnis Ithaci clamoribus actus,
 Compositò rumpit vocem, et me destinat aræ.
 Assensere omnes; et, quæ sibi quisque timebat,
 Unius in miseri exitium conversa tulere.
 Jamque dies infanda aderat; mihi sacra parari,
 Et salsæ fruges, et circum tempora vittæ.

Though Sinon in whose mouth the above passage is put, was an impostor, yet the poet intends to refer his readers to what had often happened among the Greeks, and to cruel and bloody rites long established. When they sacrificed, the sacred fillets were bound upon the heads of the idol, the victim, and the priest. The salted cake was placed upon the head of the victim. It was called "mola," hence immolare, in later times was used to signify any kind of sacrifice. The sacred fillets and salted cake may be seen on the head of the idol above described. The Greeks borrowed many things from the Persians, with whom they had many wars and considerable intercourse. The Persians derived many of their ideas from the Hindoos.

savage, the Hindoos and southern Tartars were well acquainted with most of the useful arts. The former lived in the vicinity of our continent, and probably found their way hither at an early day, while the latter came at a later period, bringing along with them the arts, the idols, and religious rites of Hisdostan, China, and the Crimea. The ancestors of our North American Indians were mere hunters, while the authors of our tumuli were shepherds and husbandmen. The temples, altars, and sacred places of the Hindoos, were always situated on the bank of some stream of water. The same observation applies to the temples, altars and sacred places of those who erected our tumuli. To the consecrated streams of Hindostan, devotees assembled from all parts of the empire, to worship their gods, and purify themselves by bathing in the sacred water. In this country, their sacred places were uniformly on the bank of some river; and who knows but that the Muskingum, the Scioto, the Miami, the Ohio, the Cumberland, and the Missisippi, were once deemed as sacred, and their banks as thickly settled, and as well cultivated, as are now the Indus, the Ganges, and the Burrampooter?

Ablution, from the situation of all the works which appear to have been devoted to sacred uses, was a rite as religiously observed by the authors of our idols, as it was neglected by our North American Indians. If the coincidences between the worship of our people, and that of the Hindoos and southern Tartars, furnish no evidence of a common origin, then I am no judge of the nature and weight of testimony.

Some years since, a clay vessel was discovered about twenty feet below the surface, in alluvial earth, in digging a well near Nashville, Tennessee. This piece of pottery was found standing on a rock, from whence a spring of water issued. This vessel was taken to Mr. Peale's museum at Philadelphia, where it now is, as I am informed. It contains about one gallon; is circular, with a flat bottom, from which it rises in a somewhat globose form, terminating at the summit with the figure of a female head. The only hole in the vessel is situated towards the summit of the globular part of it. The features of the face of the female are Asiatick. The crown of the head is covered by a cap of a pyramidical figure, with a flattened, circular summit, ending at the apex, with a round button. The ears are large, extending as low as the chin. The features resemble many of those engraved for Raffle's History; and the cap resembles Asiatick head dresses. The foregoing was taken from an essay in the "Western Review," written by Mr. John D. Clifford.

Here is farther proof of the derivation of these people from Hindostan. The features of the face; the manner of covering the head; the shape of the vessel; the religious uses to which it was probably put at this primitive, and once clear fountain, in performing ablutions, all tend to confirm us in such a belief. Could all these things have so happened, had the authors originated any where else?

[An Idol, of which this is a correct miniature, was, a few years since, dug up in Natchez, Missisippi, on a piece of ground, where, according to tradition, long before Europeans visited this country, stood an Indian Temple.

This idol is of stone; is nineteen inches in height, nine inches in width, and seven inches thick, at the extremities.

It was presented to the American Antiquarian Society, at the request of the owner, James Thompson, Esq. of Natchez, by the Hon. Winthrop Sargent.]

At what Period did these People come into the Territory now included in Ohio.

That it was in an early age of the world, we infer from the rude state of many of the arts among them.

In Italy we behold, on every side, the vestiges of a once powerful and polished people. We see the remains of roads, on which millions have trodden; of aqueducts, which supplied populous cities with water; of amphitheatres, once filled with thousands of admiring spectators of publick exhibitions.— Among the ruins of some unhappy town, we find the bust of the hero, or the god, which the chisel of the artist has polished; the canvas which the painter has made to glow with almost real life.— There, also, we find the parchment on which the poet, the biographer, the orator, and the historian have written; conveying down to us exalted ideas of their learning, their acquaintance with the arts, their genius, their eloquence, their wealth, their grandeur, and their glory.

Where, in the extended regions of the west, do we find the remains of an "Appian" or "Emilian Way?" Where do we find the moss grown column of the stately palace, the lofty dome, the solemn temple, the ruins of baths, the fragments of amphitheatres? Where the parchment on which the poet, the orator, the biographer or the historian has written, conveying down to us exalted ideas of the learning, the genius, the morals, the virtues, the wealth, the eloquence, the military prowess, the power, the grandeur, and glory of that people, or their acquaintance with the arts and sciences? Where find we the bust which the statuary has polished? Where the painting of the artist?

If that people had axes like ours, Why do we find so many of stone? If they had mirrours of glass like ours, Why use those of isinglass? If they manufactured hemp, flax, cotton and wool, Why use the bark of trees and birds' feathers in their dress? If they had the art of polishing the precious stones which they wore as ornaments, Why are so many rock crystals, in their natural state, found in our mounds? Proofs of primitive times are seen in their manners and customs; in their modes of burial and worship; in their wells, which resemble those of the patriarchal ages. Here the reader has only to recollect the one at Marietta, those at Portsmouth, on Paint Creek, at Cincinnati, and compare them with those described in Genesis. Jacob rolled the stone from the well's mouth; Rachel descended with her pitcher, and brought up water for her future husband, and for the flocks of her father.

Before men were acquainted with letters, they raised monuments of unwrought fragments of rocks, for the purpose of perpetuating the memory of events; such are here. In the patriarchal ages, men were in the habit of burying on high places and in mounds; so did this people. *They* buried in caves; so did *these*. Caves have been found, near Gallipolis, near Greenupsburg, in Kentucky, and in many other places in the hilly region of Ohio and the country adjacent. In some of these, skeletons have been discovered.

Their military works are such as any people would erect, who had just passed from the first to the second, from the hunter to the pastoral state of society. Were they not here as early as the days of Abraham and Lot? The geology of the country throws a faint beam of light upon the dark path, in which we are groping along with cautious steps.

The line of forts already mentioned, on the authority of Governour Clinton, beginning at the mouth of Cataraugus Creek, may be referred to. These forts, if forts they were, were built upon the brow of the hill, which appears to have once been the southern shore of lake Erie. Since they were built, the waters of the Erie have receded.

These works are from three to five miles from the present shore, and the surface is covered by a vegetable mould, made from the decomposition and decay of vegetables, six, eight and ten inches in depth. Governour Clinton, in his Memoir, justly observes, that it must have taken a long time for a forest to grow on the earth, after it had been laid bare by the recession of the waters of the lake.—The seeds of plants must have been carried there by the wind and the birds; and, at this time, no difference is observed between this and the surrounding woods.

William Coleman, Esq. of Euclid, Ohio, a very observing and intelligent man, who was one of the first settlers on the lake shore, has never found any of these works north of the northern ridge; and recollects but two or three between the first and second ridges, and these were small. Compare these facts with the following.

In Pickaway and Ross counties, the vegetable mould covering the works of this class, is not generally more than four inches in thickness; and some of them are situated on alluvions so low, that their bases are sometimes wet by high freshets. There is such a work on the interval, near the Scioto at Circleville; there are some thus situated in Ross county, and numbers on the Great Miami.

Many of these works had gateways and parallel walls, leading down to creeks which once washed the foot of hills, from whence the streams have now receded, formed extensive and newer alluvions, and worn down their channels, in some instances, ten and even fifteen feet. We refer the reader to the works on the waters of Licking, a drawing and description of which are given.

There is a work near Colonel Dunlap's, in Ross county, where there was a way which led to a low piece of ground, that, from appearances, was once covered by the waters of a pond, which appear to have been dried away for centuries past.

The botany of the country has been consulted on this subject. It would have taken some time for the seeds of plants and trees to have been completely scattered over a whole country, extensively cultivated by a considerable population. Now, the only difference between the botany of the country where the works are found, and those tracts where there are none, is, that the trees are the largest on and about the works. Trees of the largest size, whose concentrick annular rings have been counted, have, in many instances, as many as four hundred, and they appear to be at least the third growth since the works were occupied.

An examination of the works themselves may throw some light on the subject. Those along the lakes are comparatively few in number and small in size, but increase in both respects, greatly, as their authors proceeded towards the south. Their numbers must have wonderfully increased as they slowly descended the water courses, and their improvement in the useful arts is every where visible.

Their pottery at Salem, on the shore of lake Erie, was rude, and but ill calculated for the purposes for which it was intended; whilst along the Ohio, some of it is equal to any thing of the kind now manufactured. Along lake Erie, it was not glazed, nor was it polished; on the Ohio, it was well glazed or polished, and the vessels well shaped. Ornaments of silver, or copper, certainly belonging to this people, have not been found north of Newark; whereas below that place, vast numbers have been discovered.

North of the last mentioned place, I know of no wells perforated through rocks, by them; near that place, a great number are seen dug through as hard rocks as any in the country.

How long did this People reside here?

That they lived here for a long time, appears evident from the very numerous cemeteries, and the vast numbers of persons of all ages who were here buried. It is highly probable that more persons were buried in these mounds than now live in this state. They lived in towns, many of which were populous, especially along the Scioto from Columbus, southward.

Their greatest settlements in Ohio, were on Paint Creek, a few miles from Chillicothe; at Circleville; and along the very banks of the Ohio river, especially near Grave Creek, and the mouths of the Muskingum and Scioto. Some have supposed, that they were driven away by powerful foes; but appearances by no means justify this supposition.— That they contended against some people to the northeast of them is evident; but that they leisurely moved down the streams, is also evident, from their increased numbers, and their improvement in the knowledge of the arts. These required time and a settled state of society.

That they came here after the Indians had settled themselves along the Atlantick coast, is inferred from the greater knowledge of the arts diffused among the former than the latter.

It is among a dense population that these improvements are effected. It is here, that necessity, the mother of invention, prompts man to subject such animals to his dominion as he discovers most docile, best calculated to assist him in his labours, and supply him with food and raiment. From a hunter he becomes a shepherd, and drives before him his numerous flocks, weds the vine to the elm, raises pulse and maize, and constructs a better cabin for himself and family to protect them from the inclemencies of the weather. As the population increases, he subjects an additional number of animals to his dominion, and cultivates an additional number of indigenous plants. He improves the breeds of his animals already domesticated; renders his implements of industry more perfect, and extends the field of cultivation. At length the mechanick arts become so necessary, that some persons devote their whole time to them, whilst others exchange their own articles of trade for those belonging to the people of neighbouring nations. They find this exchange mutually profitable; and the profession of the merchant becomes honourable. The ship is constructed in place of the bark canoe; numbers dwell on the mountain wave, and make the deep their home. The arts and sciences are cultivated; man puts off his rough savage manners, and lays aside, by degrees, the ignorance and prejudices attendant on such a state of society. He has now arrived at the third, highest and last state of society —the mercantile.

Laws and municipal regulations are multiplied to protect man against man, the weak against the strong, the artless against the artful, the poor and the oppressed against the wealthy oppressor, the person of fair fame against the slanderer's tongue; arts are improved; science flourishes. This is the natural order of things. Their not having attained to this height in the scale of civilization, is one proof that the authors of our Antiquities lived in the earlier ages of the world; but they evidently improved in their condition while residing here. To have thus improved and multiplied, required time.

How great a Number of this People inhabited this Country?

We cannot arrive at absolute certainty on this subject, but we can examine their works, whose ruins we every where behold. We can examine their graves; but no historian has been left to inform us; no ghost will rise to tell us; and no response to his questions on this head, is heard by him who knocks at their tombs. Mr. Brackenridge has conjectured, that there were once five thousand villages of this people in the valley of the Missisippi. I have never counted them, nor has any other person; but the state of Ohio was once much thicker settled, in all probability, than it now is, when it contains about seven hundred thousand inhabitants. Many of the mounds contain an immense number of skeletons. Those of Big Grave Creek are believed to be completely filled with human bones. The large ones, all along the principal rivers in this state, are also filled with skeletons. Millions of human beings have been buried in these tumuli. To have supported such a great population, the inhabitants must have been considerably employed in agriculture.

From the Rocky Mountains in the west, to the Alleghanies in the east, the country must have been more or less settled by them; and the number of people after their settlements reached the Ohio river, must have been far greater than is generally supposed. To have erected such works, so numerous and large, must have required a great population.

The STATE of the ARTS among them.

Some ideas on this subject may be gathered from the foregoing accounts of their works.

That they manufactured bricks, and very good ones too, we know from the discoveries made on opening their tumuli; in not a few of which, bricks have been found, besides those already described.

Gold ornaments are said to have been found in several tumuli; but I have never seen any.

Silver, very well plated, has been found in several mounds, besides those at Circleville and Marietta.

Copper, has been found in more than twenty mounds, but generally not very well wrought. It is in all cases, like that described by Dr. Drake, already quoted. The copper, belonging to the sword, found at Marietta, is wrought with the most art of any which I have seen.

Pipe bowls of copper, hammered out, and not welded together, but lapped over, have been found in many tumuli. General Tupper described such an one to me, found by him on the elevated square at Marietta, or rather a few feet below the surface of that work. Similar ones have been discovered in other places. A bracelet of copper was found in a stone mound near Chillicothe, and forwarded to the museum at Cincinnati by the Hon. Jessup N. Couch, Esq. some time since. This was a rude ornament, and resembled somewhat the link of a common log chain; the ends passed by each other, but were not welded together. I have seen several arrow heads of this metal, some of which were five or six inches in length, and must have been used as heads of spears. Circular medals of this metal, several inches in diameter, very thin and much injured by time, have often been found in the tumuli. They had no inscriptions that I could discover. Some of them were large enough to have answered for breast plates. The small copper kettles, sometimes found near lake Erie, belonged to Indians, and were derived from the French and other Europeans.

Iron has been found in very few instances, having oxydized. They made use of it in some cases for knives and swords, the remains of which have been discovered in many tumuli. The balls found sometimes in alluvial earth, and in mounds, supposed by some to be cannon balls of iron, are not the work of art, but martial pyrites. I have seen very beautiful ones taken from ancient works in this country. Of *cast* iron, I have seen no article belonging to that people.

Glass has not been found, belonging certainly to that people, within my knowledge. Those pieces which have been discovered, owe their origin to the people who now live here.

Their mirrors were of isinglass, (mica membranacea) and have been met with in fifty places, at least, within my own knowledge. Besides the large and very elegant one at Circleville, and the fragments at Cincinnati, I have found more or less of these mirrors in almost all the mounds which have been opened in the country. They were common among that people, and answered very well the purpose for which they were intended. These mirrors were very thick, otherwise they would not have reflected the light.

I am disposed to believe, although their houses in some instances might have been built of stone and brick, as in the walled town on Paint Creek, and some few other places, yet that their habitations were of wood, or that they dwelt in tents; otherwise their ruins would be more frequently met with in every part of this great country. Along the Ohio, where the river is in many places wearing and washing away its banks, hearths and fireplaces are brought to light, two, four and even six feet below the surface. A long time must have elapsed, since the earth was deposited over them. Those who wish to see these fireplaces and remains of chimnies, by examining the bank of the Muskingum at its mouth, at Point Harmar, opposite Marietta, may gratify their curiosity. These fireplaces resemble very much those belonging to the rude cabins of the first settlers, in this or any other part of the United States. Around them are deposited immense quantities of muscle shells, bones of animals, &c. From the depth of many of these remains of chimnies, below the present surface of the earth, on which, at the settlement of this country by its present inhabitants, grew as large trees as any in the surrounding forest, the conclusion is, that a long period, perhaps of a thousand years, has elapsed since these hearths were deserted.

Scites which had been occupied by mills moved by water; buildings for manufactories of any kind of stone, I have not seen.

Some have thought that they had discovered cellars, on the scites of ancient towns. WELLS have been found in many places, and they are such as we read of in the patriarchal ages. Those at Marietta, near Portsmouth, and four on Paint Creek, are particularly referred to.

The potter's ware is by far the most interesting of any of their manufactures. On the surface of the earth, or very near it, a rude kind of ware, made of sand stone and clay in composition, near lake Erie; of clay, on the northern waters of the Scioto; of clay and shells in composition, on the Ohio and Missisippi, is frequently found, belonging to a recent era, and manufactured even by the present race of Indians. None of this ware is glazed, and its workmanship is rude. But at the bottom of mounds, or near the head of some distinguished personage, vessels are found in some instances equal to any now manufactured in any part of the world. These are not always made of the same materials. Two covers of vessels were found in a stone mound in Ross county, in this state, very ingeniously wrought by the artist, and highly polished. These were made of a calcareous breccia; fragments of which were examined by Professor Silliman, of Yale College, Connecticut. These covers resembled almost exactly, and were quite equal to vessels of that material manufactured in Italy at the present time.

An urn* was found in a mound, a few miles from Chillicothe, a drawing of which follows. It is three sevenths of the size of the article each way.

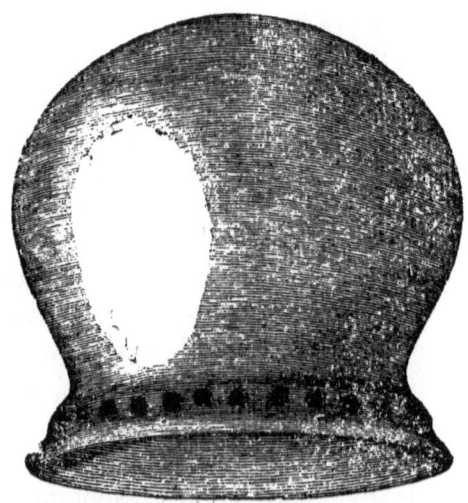

* Now in the possession of Mr. J. W. Collet, Chillicothe, Ohio.

This urn very much resembles one found in a similar work in Scotland, and mentioned by Pennant in his Tour.* The urn there described was thirteen inches high, and of a blackish appearance, as if it had been filled with oil. It was found in a tumulus near Bamff, and contained arrow heads, ashes and calcined bones.

These urns generally contain human bones which have been burnt in a hot fire; and, from the appearance of the vessels, oil of some kind has been put into them with the bones.

Some of these urns appear to have been made of a composition resembling that of which mortars for physicians and apothecaries are now manufactured by Europeans. There is such a one now in existence, and in the possession of a gentleman residing on the little Scioto, in Scioto county, Ohio. It contains about three quarts; is brought to a perfect point at the bottom. About half way from the top to the bottom is a groove around its outside, and two ears, through which a chain may be inserted, by which to suspend it. It was found twelve feet below the surface of the earth, in the alluvion on the Ohio river. It had on it marks of fire, and is not injured by exposure to considerable heat.

A small vessel is now in the possession of S. Williams, Esq. of Chillicothe, which it is supposed might have been used as a crucible. A drawing of it, of about half the size, each way, is here annexed.

* Vol. I. page 154. London, fourth edition, 1790.

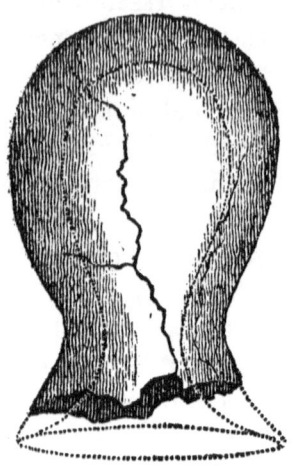

It was found in a tumulus, eight miles from the last mentioned place. It has on it the marks of fire; and bears as great a degree of heat, as the pots now used in glass manufactories, and is made of the same kind of clay.

Dr. Hildreth has described several articles which he has seen; one of which, was a vessel which contained about two quarts. It was handsomely proportioned, and nearly in the form of a cocoa nut shell. It had four neat handles placed near the brim, and opposite each other. It was found in the bank of an island near Belpre. On the beach, near the mouth of Muskingum, was discovered a curious ornament. It is made of white marble, in form a circle, about three inches in diameter. The outer edge is about one inch in thickness with a narrow rim. The sides are deeply concave, and in the centre is a hole about half an inch in diameter. It is beautifully finished, and so smooth, that Dr.

Hildreth is of the opinion that it was once highly polished. It is now in the possession of David Putnam, Esq. of Marietta, Ohio.

Other articles, similar to this, have been found in several mounds in many places. The use to which the one described was put, cannot certainly be known. Was it a rude wind instrument of musick? or, Was it a badge of office and distinction?

Some of their arrow and spear heads are brought to such fine and long points, so perfectly regular, that it is difficult to ascertain how they were made, even with steel instruments. Mr. Clifford has heard of a fish spear, with six or seven long prongs, perfectly separated, barbed and carved out of calcedonick flint.

I have an axe in my little cabinet, found near Jackson, in this state, and presented to me by Daniel Hoffman, Esq. made of a species of green stone, equal to Egyptian granite. It is polished in the neatest manner.

Mr. Clifford has a pipe in his collection, which was found in digging a trench on Sandusky river, in alluvial earth, six feet below the surface, which displays great taste in its execution. The rim of the bowl is in high relief, and the front represents a handsome female face. The stone from which it is made, is the real talc graphique, exactly resembling the stone of which the Chinese make their IDOLS. No talc of this species is known to exist on this side of the Alleghanies; and this article, of course, must have been brought here from a distance, probably from Asia.

Fragments of fishing nets and mocasons, made of a species of rattle weed, have been found in the nitrous caves of Kentucky.

The mummies have generally been found enveloped in three coverings; first, in a coarse species of linen cloth, of about the consistency and texture of cotton bagging. It was evidently woven by the same kind of process, which is still practised in the interiour parts of Africa. The warp being extended by some slight kind of machinery, the woof was passed across it, and then twisted every two threads of the warp together, before the second passage of the filling. This seems to have been the first rude method of weaving in Asia, Africa and America. The second envelope of the mummies, is a kind of net work, of coarse threads, formed of very small, loose meshes, in which were fixed the feathers of various kinds of birds, so as to make a perfectly smooth surface, lying all in one direction. The art of this tedious, but beautiful, manufacture was well understood in Mexico, and still exists on the northwest coast of America, and in the islands of the Pacifick ocean. In those isles, it is the state or court dress. The third and outer envelope of these mummies is either like the one first described, or it consists of leather, sewed together. My authority is Mr. Clifford, of Lexington, Kentucky, a member of the American Antiquarian Society.

This account of manufactured articles of similar vessels, made of our best clays, might be extended to many pages, but it is hoped that what has been said, may suffice. I beg leave, however, to add, that the ancient inhabitants of the west, were better acquainted with the manufacture of vessels of this kind, than with almost any other articles. Though they had some few very well manufactured swords and knives of iron, possibly of steel, yet they certainly used many stone axes, stone knives, arrow heads, &c. which are found in many of the tumuli. Stones curiously wrought and well polished of granite, of hornblend, of marble, of calcareous breccia, and sometimes of sand stone, are discovered in tumuli; a collection of which, I have before me. Several drawings of these are given. Rock crystals, of the most beautiful species, were probably worn as ornaments, one of which I have in my possession.

Drawings of Ornaments and Domestick Utensils, taken from Mounds, chiefly by Caleb Atwater, and most of them in his possession.

All these drawings are three fifths each way as large as the article they represent.

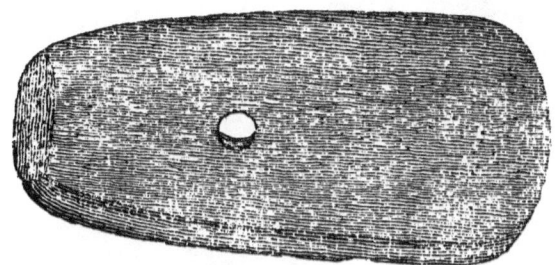

A stone ornament, supposed to have been worn on the breast, suspended by a string round the wearer's neck.

A Stone Axe.

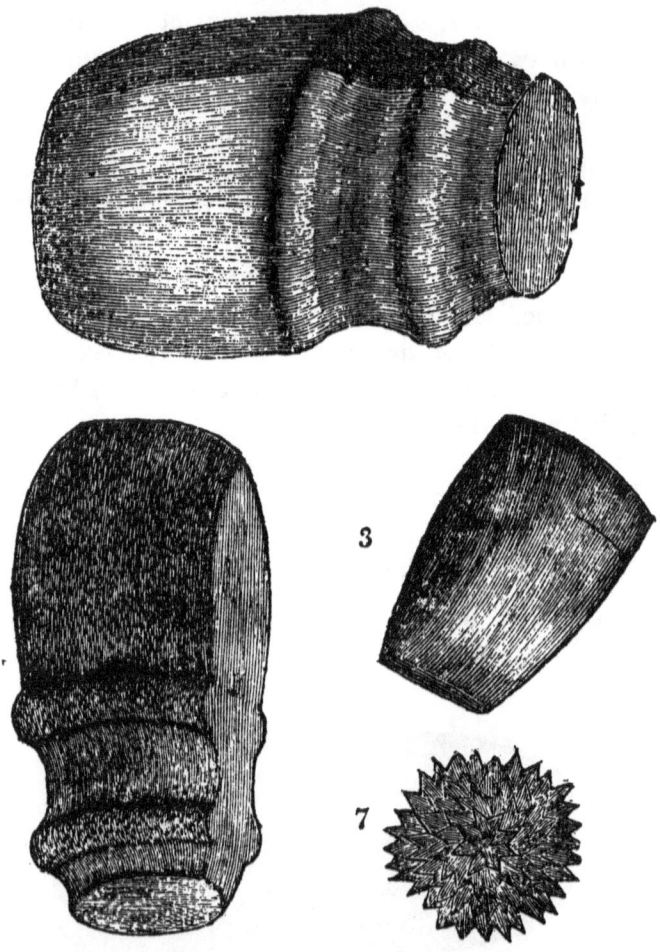

3. A small Axe of granite. 5. A curious stone Axe, of granite. 7. A beautiful Rock Crystal, supposed to have been worn as an ornament.

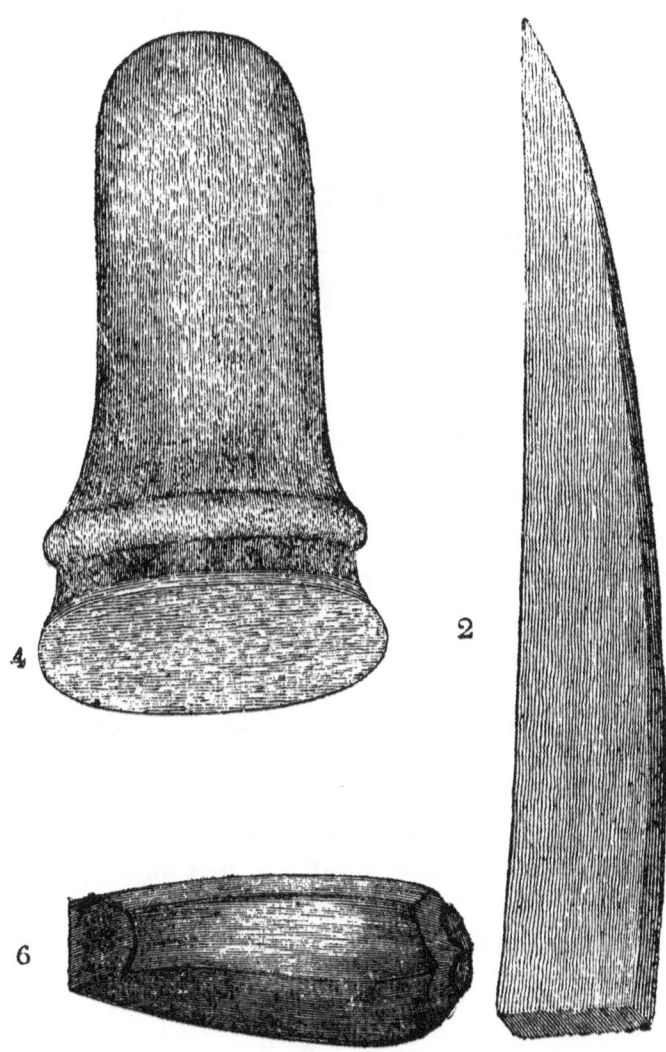

2. An ancient Pickaxe, made of hornblend.—
4. A stone Pestle, of granite. 6. Stone Axe.

[The following is a drawing (a little less than one third of the size, each way) of an Indian Stone Axe, ploughed up in a field, in Eastwindsor, Connecticut, belonging to Mr. Abner Reed.]

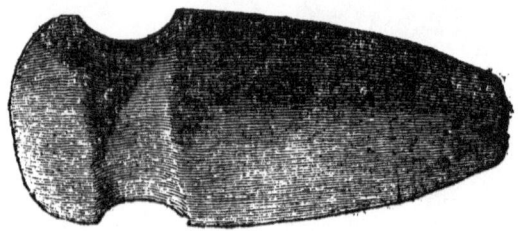

It is evident, from the articles which have been ploughed up in the field above mentioned, and those adjacent, that there was once in this place, a settlement of the Aboriginals. The articles found were axes, of granite; a very large number of arrow heads, of flint; pieces of pots, made of chalk stone; and other domestick articles of stone.

Several axes, similar in shape to the one above mentioned, and others shaped differently, found in the Newengland States, together with some from Missisippi, and others from the Choctaw country; with many other domestick utensils, all of stone, of various kinds, manufactured in former times by the native Indians, are deposited in the Cabinet of the American Antiquarian Society.]

Whether our ancient people used clothing made of flax, hemp or cotton, I do not know; but mats made of something resembling hemp, or possibly the bark of some kind of vegetable, have been found, besides the one mentioned in the account of the mound once standing in Chillicothe. These articles are so much injured by time, that it is quite difficult to say, with certainty, of what materials they were made.

No article has been found, within my knowledge, which contained on it either letters or hieroglyphicks. Several stories to the contrary, have been propagated, but, on inquiry, they had no foundation in truth.

No BRASS has been discovered here, it is believed.

Smoking pipes, made of stone, of clay, &c. have often been found; and the teeth of many of the fossil skulls, show that their owners were in the constant habit of using them.

SCIENTIFICK ACQUIREMENTS.

The manner in which their works are almost always planned, when thoroughly examined, have furnished matter of admiration to all intelligent persons who have attended to the subject.

Nearly all the lines of ancient works found in the whole country, where the form of the ground admits of it, are right ones, pointing to the four cardinal points. Where there are mounds enclosed, the gateways are most frequently on the east side of the works towards the rising sun. Where the situation admits of it, in military works, the openings are generally towards one or more of the cardinal points. Had their authors no knowledge of astronomy? These things never could have so happened, with such invariable exactness in almost all cases, without some design.

On the whole, I am convinced, from an attention to many hundreds of these works, in every part of the west which I have visited, that their authors had some knowledge of astronomy. The pastoral life, which men followed in the early ages, was certainly very favourable to the attainment of such a knowledge. Dwelling in tents, or in the open air, with the heavenly bodies in full view, and much more liable to suffer from any change in the weather than we are, who dwell in comfortable habitations, they would of course, direct their attention to the prognosticks of approaching heat and cold, stormy or pleasant weather. Our own sailors are an example in point. Let a person, even wholly unaccustomed to the seas, be wafted for a few weeks by the winds and waves, and he is all ear to every breeze, all eye to every part of the heavens. Thus, in the earliest ages of mankind, astronomy was attended to, partly from necessity; hence a knowledge of this science was early diffused among men, the proofs of which are beheld in their works, not only here, but in every part of the globe where they then dwelt. It was reserved for the immortal geniuses of modern times, to make the most astonishing discoveries in this science, aided by a knowledge of figures, and an acquaintance with the telescope; but men in ancient times were by no means inattentive to this noble science.

Their Religious Rites and Places of Worship.

Knowledge on these subjects must be sought for in and about the mounds, which appear to have been used for many important purposes.

In addition to what is already said, under the descriptions of mounds, we will here add, that on the Cany fork of Cumberland river, a vessel was found in an ancient work, about four feet below the surface, a drawing of which is here given.* It is believed to be an exact likeness.

The object itself may be thus described. It consists of three heads, joined together at the back part of them, near the top, by a stem or handle, which rises above the heads about three inches. This stem is hollow, six inches in circumference at the top, increasing in size as it descends. These heads are all of the same dimensions, being about four inches from the top to the chin. The face at the eyes is three inches broad, decreasing in breadth

* The original drawing was by Miss Sarah Clifford, of Lexington, Kentucky. It is by some, called a "Triune Idol."

all the way to the chin. All the strong marks of the Tartar countenance are distinctly preserved, and expressed with so much skill, that even a modern artist might be proud of the performance. The countenances are all different each from the other, and denote an old person and two younger ones.

The face of the eldest is painted around the eyes with yellow, shaded with a streak of the same colour, beginning from the top of the ear, running in a semicircular form to the ear on the other side of the head. Another painted line begins at the lower part of the eye, and runs down before each ear about one inch. [*See figure* 1.]

Back view.

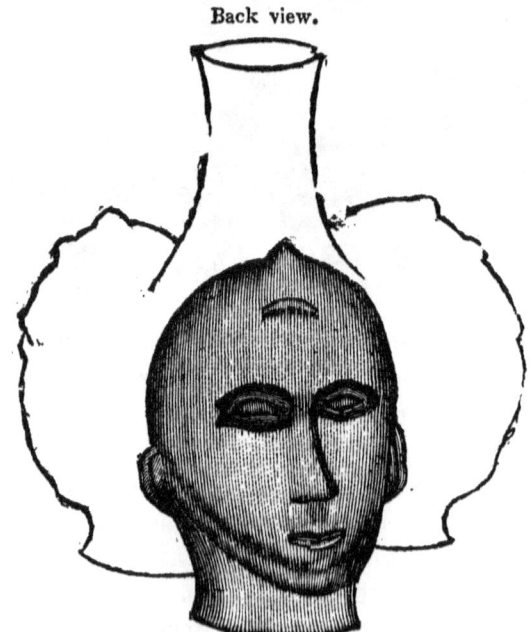

The second represents a person of a grave countenance, much younger than the preceding one,

painted very differently and of a different colour.—
A streak of reddish brown surrounds each eye.—
Another line of the same colour, beginning at the
top of one ear, passes under the chin, and ends at
the top of the other ear. The ears also are slightly
tinged with the same colour. [*See figure* 2.]

The third, [*figure* 3.] in its characteristical features, resembles the others, representing one of the Tartar family. The whole of the face is slightly tinged with vermilion, or some paint resembling it. Each cheek has a spot on it, of the size of a quarter of a dollar, brightly tinged with the same paint. On the chin is a similar spot. One circumstance worthy of remark is, that though these colours must have been exposed to the damp earth for many centuries, they have, nothwithstanding, preserved every shade in all its brilliancy.

This "Triune vessel" stands upon three necks, which are about an inch and a half in length. The whole is composed of a fine clay, of a light umber colour, which has been rendered hard by the action of fire. The heads are hollow, and the vessel contains about one quart.

Does it not represent the three chief gods of India, Brahma, Vishnoo and Siva? Let the reader look at the plate representing this vessel, and consult the "Asiatic Researches," by Sir William Jones; let him also read Buchanan's "Star in the East," and the accounts there found of the idolatry of the Hindoos; and, unless his mind is formed differently from mine, he will see in this idol, one proof at least, that the people who raised our ancient works, were idolators; and, that some of them worshipped gods resembling the three principal deities of India. What tends to strengthen this inference, is, that nine murex shells, the same as described by Sir William Jones in " Asiatic Researches," and by Symmes in his " Embassy to Ava," have been found within twenty miles of Lexington, Kentucky, in an ancient work. Their component parts remained unchanged, and they were every way in an excellent state of preservation. These shells, so rare in India, are highly esteemed and consecrated to their god Mahadeva, whose character is the same with the Neptune of Greece and Rome. This shell, among the Hindoos, is the musical instrument of their Tritons. These shells, found near Lexington, are in the musuem of Mr. John D. Clifford, of that place, a very worthy gentleman. The foot of the Siamese god, Gaudma or Boodh, is represented by a sculpture, in Ava, of six feet in length, and the toes are carved, each to represent a shell of the murex. These shells have been found in many mounds which have been opened in every part of this country; and this is a proof that a considerable value was set upon them by their owners.

That the people who erected our ancient works were idolators, is inferred also from the age of the world in which they lived; from the certainty which history, sacred and profane, affords, that all other nations were idolators at the same time; that all people, except the Jews, who buried their dead in tumuli, were idolators.

Many of the most intelligent persons, who have examined our antiquities with care, have expressed a belief that the sun was worshipped by this people. Without pretending to decide on a subject so intricate, and where there is no positive proof of the fact; and without even expressing an opinion myself, the circumstances on which others have founded such an opinion shall be briefly stated.

Wherever there is a walk like a road up to any large mound, elevated, circular or square work, where the situation of the ground will admit of it, such works are uniformly on the east side, as at Circleville. Mounds are generally so situated, as to afford a good view of the rising sun. Hundreds might be mentioned as examples. Where mounds are encircled with walls and ditches, if there is a gateway, it is almost uniformly towards the east. Where persons belonging to this people were buried in caves, as they sometimes were, the mouth of the cave is towards the east; wherever we find a pavement in a semicircular form, partly enclosing a mound, it is always on the east side. When persons were buried in graves, as they often were,* these graves were east and west. I suspect that our custom of burying the dead in the same way, was derived from the same origin; and our practice of having our burying grounds always near churches, and sometimes under them, is derived from the primitive custom of interring the dead either near or in the ancient tumuli, which were us-

* Many wonderful tales have been related of a race of pigmies, whose burying grounds have been discovered in the West. A little more attention would have cleared up the mystery. The legs below the knee joint were turned under the body, which made the graves very short, though the skeletons are as large as those found in our mounds. They were a short but very thickset people.

ed as altars, on which temples were, in later ages, erected.

Medals, representing the sun with its rays of light, have been found in the mounds. One of these was discovered by Judge Crull, of Scioto county, Ohio, a fragment of which was forwarded, to be deposited in the Cabinet of the American Antiquarian Society. It is made of a very fine clay, and coloured in the composition before it was hardened by heat. It was originally more than three inches in diameter.

But it appears to me, judging from the same, or rather similar, data, there is quite as much evidence of their worshipping the moon; for the semicircles represent the new moon; and copper medals, perfectly round, thin, flat and smooth, without any thing to represent rays of light, have been much oftener found than any others; and semicircular works, sometimes three or more joined together, always however facing the east, are to be seen entirely unconnected with any other works. There are several such not far from Col. James Dunlap's, in Ross county. They are of earth, and only a few feet high, as described to me by the above named gentleman. Such works are quite common where this people once dwelt. I have sometimes suspected them to be unfinished works, where mounds were about to be erected on the west side of the semicircles.

All I pretend to do, is to lay an unvarnished statement of facts before the reader, who can form what opinion he chooses on the subject.

What finally became of this People? and, Where are their Descendents now?

On opening a mound near the " Big Grave" below Wheeling, a few years since, a stone was found, haying on it a brand exactly similar to the one most commonly used by the Mexicans in marking their cattle and horses. The above fact is noticed by Harris in his 'Tour,' to which the reader is referred.

The head of the sus-tajassu, or Mexican hog, cut off square, was found in a saltpetre cave in Kentucky, a few years since, by Dr. Brown. This circumstance is mentioned by Dr. Drake, in his "Picture of Cincinnati." The nitre had preserved it. It had been deposited there by the ancient inhabitants, where it must have laid for many centuries. I am not aware of this animal's being found north of Mexico. The presumption is, that the ancient inhabitants took these animals along with them, in their migrations, until they finally settled themselves in Mexico. Other animals were, in all probability, domesticated by them, and taken with them also.

Our ancient works continue all the way into Mexico, increasing indeed in size, number and grandeur, but preserving the same forms, and appear to have been put to the same uses. The form of our works is round, square, semicircular, octagonal, &c. agreeing in all these respects with the works in Mexico. The first works built by the Mexicans were mostly of earth, and not much superiour to the common ones on the Missisippi.

Temples were afterwards erected on the elevated squares, circles, &c. but were still, like ours, surrounded by walls of earth.

These sacred places, in Mexico, were called "Teocalli," which, in the vernacular tongue of the most ancient tribe of Mexicans, signifies "Mansions of the gods." They included within their sacred walls, gardens, fountains, habitations of priests, temples, altars, and magazines of arms. This circumstance may account for many things which have excited some surprize among those who have hastily visited the works on Paint Creek, those at Portsmouth, Marietta, Circleville, Newark, &c.

It is doubted by many to what uses these works were put; whether they were used as forts, as cemeteries, as altars, as temples, &c.: whereas, they contained all these either within their walls, or were intimately connected with them. Many persons cannot imagine why the works, at the places above mentioned, were so extensive, complicated, differing so much in form, size and elevation among themselves. They contained within them altars, temples, cemeteries, habitations of priests, gardens, wells, fountains, places devoted to sacred purposes of various kinds, and the whole of their arms, except such as were in immediate use. They were calculated for defence, and were resorted to in cases of the last necessity. When driven to these, their authors fought with the greatest desperation. We are warranted in this conclusion, by knowing that these works are exactly similar to the most ancient ones now to be seen in Mexico; connected with the fact, that the Mexican works did contain within them ALL that we have above stated.

The " Teocalli" are attributed, by the Mexicans, to the Aztecks, who settled in Mexico in the year 648. Teocalli, Humboldt says, is derived from the name of one of the gods, to which they were dedicated, Tezcatlipoca, the Brahma of the Mexicans.

The pyramid of Cholula was seated on a tumulus, with four stages, and was dedicated to the god of the air, Quetzalcoatl. Our Teocalli in Ohio have generally but one stage, as at Circleville, Marietta, and Portsmouth. Others have two, as the one described already, on Paint Creek; and there is one, according to H. M. Brackenridge, Esq. near St. Louis, with three stages. That in process of time, when their numbers had wonderfully increased, they should raise a tumulus with four stages, is not remarkable. If temples of wood had been erected upon the summits of our elevated squares, no traces of them now would be seen. Time would have long since effaced them.

Their religious rites were, it is believed, the same as those of Mexico and Peru. We wish not to repeat what we have said already, but cannot help referring to the fact of the numerous mirrors of *mica membranacea*, (isinglass) which have been found in the mounds situated within round and square circumvallations. The one at Circleville was quite entire, and pieces of others have been found in nearly all other tumuli similarly situated, wherever they have been opened. That they were used as mirrors, appears highly probable from their shape and size. One of the three principal gods of the South Americans was called by a name which signifies, "The god of the shining mirror." He was supposed to be a god who reflected his own supreme perfections, and was represented by a mirror, which was made in that country of polished obsidian, or of mica like ours. The scarcity of obsidian, which is a volcanick production, may well account for its absence in this country; the numerous volcanoes in South America equally account for the abundance of mirrors of obsidian there. This deity was represented as enjoying perpetual youth and beauty. Other gods had images placed on pedestals in the Mexican temples; this one had a mirror on his. This divinity was held in awful veneration, as the great unknown God of the universe. Who does not here discover a strong trace of a knowledge of the true God, derived by tradition from the first patriarchs?

Clavigero, who was well acquainted with the histories of the Mexicans and Peruvians, professes to point out the places from whence they emigrated; the several places they stopped at; and the times which they continued to sojourn there. According to him, they finally arrived in Mexico in 648, and came across the Pacifick not far from Behring's streights, and did not come as far to the eastward as Ohio. Some tribes might arrive there by the route pointed out by him; numbers might have come this way, and have tarried here for thousands of years. Others might have found their way into South America, by crossing the Pacifick at different places and at various times. Greenlanders have been driven upon the coast of Ireland. Thus transported by winds and waves, by stress of weather, man has found the islands in the Pacifick.

In the same way, might have arrived persons from Africa and Europe. Austral Asians, Chinese, Hindoos, Japanese, Birmans, Kamschatdales and Tartars, might have all found their way into South America at different times, and by different routes; but, that the great body of them came here, and finally emigrated into South America, is highly probable from the circumstances already mentioned. Others might be noticed, but What more is necessary? We see a line of ancient works, reaching from the south side of lake Ontario across this state, on to the banks of the Missisippi; along the banks of that river; through the upper part of the province of Texas, around the Mexican Gulph, quite into Mexico. And the evidence is as strong, when thoroughly examined, that they were erected by the same people as there would be, that a house found standing alone, on some wild and uninhabited heath, was erected by the hand of man.

It is true, that no historian has told us the names of the mighty chieftains whose ashes are inurned in our tumuli; no poet's song has been handed down to us, in which their exploits are noticed. History has not informed us, who were their priests, their orators, their ablest statesmen, or their greatest warriours. But we find idols which show that the same gods were worshipped here as in Mexico.— The works left behind them, are exactly similar to those in Mexico and Peru; and our works are continued quite into that country.

One fact I will here mention, which I have never learned was observed by any person but the writer, is, that wherever there is a group of tumuli, &c. three are uniformly larger than the rest, and stand in the most prominent places. Three such are to be seen standing in a line on the north side of Detroit river, opposite the town of Detroit.— Three such are to be seen near Athens, and at a great many places along the Ohio river. There are three such near the town of Piketon, and already described. Were they not altars dedicated to their three principal gods? Where they are all enclosed within walls, mirrors are only found in one of such tumuli. But one of the three gods of the people of Anahuac, was represented by " The Shining Mirror," which was the name of that deity.

With the remains of such of that people as were buried in any other places, except in elevated squares, circles, &c. some article, which had been dear or useful to the owner while living, is always found; but, although human bones are quite abundant, though lying without order, in such elevated places, yet no articles are found with them, except it be such, or rather the fragments of such, as were used about their sacrifices. These circumstances have induced Mr. John D. Clifford and others, who have devoted great attention to our antiquities, to believe that the fossil bones, found in such places, belonged to persons who were offered as victims upon altars devoted to the worship of cruel gods.— Such writers say, that if the bones had been honourably buried, articles of some kind would have been deposited with them.

Although I have always doubted the truth of some of the relations of the Spanish writers, respecting the persecuted people of Montezuma, there is too much reason to believe that the practice of sacrificing human beings existed among them. The Spaniards have probably exaggerated, yet I fear that they did not entirely fabricate the horrid accounts of such sacrifices. And, upon the whole, we have almost as much evidence of the existence of human sacrifices among those who built our elevated squares and works of that class, in North, as we have in South America.

Thus we have traced the authors of our ancient works, from India to North, and thence to South, America. Their works being few and small, rude and irregular at first, but increasing in number, improving in every respect as we have followed them; showing the increased numbers and improved condition of their authors, as they migrated towards the country where they finally settled.

The place from whence they came, their religious rites, the attributes of their gods, the number of their principal ones, their sacred places, their situation near some considerable stream of water, their ideas of purification by the use of water, and of atonement by sacrifice, the manner of burying their dead, and many other strong circumstances in the history of this people, as well as in that of other nations existing at the same period of time, lead us to the conclusion, that the more carefully we examine the Antiquities of this or any other country, the more evidence will be found, tending to establish the truth of the Mosaick history. The discoveries of the Antiquarian throw a strong and steady light upon the scriptures, while the scriptures afford to the Antiquarian the means of elucidating many subjects otherways difficult to be explained, and serve as an important guide in the prosecution of his investigations.

APPENDIX.

The following extracts from Humboldt's Views of the Cordilleras, &c. are subjoined, to shew the correspondence which exists between the Teocalli of the Mexicans, and the tumuli of the North Americans. The resemblance will be perceived, and is supposed to furnish evidence that they are the work of the same race of people, indicating their improvement in the arts, and their increased population as they progressed from the north to the south, and supporting the opinions respecting their origin and final destination, which have been advanced by the author of this memoir.

" Among those swarms of nations, which, from the seventh to the twelfth century of the Christian era, successively inhabited the country of Mexico, five are enumerated, the Toltecks, the Cicimecks, the Acolhuans, the Tlascaltecks, and the Aztecks, who, notwithstanding their political divisions, spoke the same language, followed the same worship, and built pyramidal edifices, which they regarded as *teocallis*, that is to say, the house of their gods.—

These edifices were all of the same form, though of very different dimensions; they were pyramids, with several terraces, and the sides of which stood exactly in the direction of the meridian, and the parallel of the place. The Teocalli was raised in the midst of a square and walled enclosure, which, somewhat like the περιβολος of the Greeks, contained gardens, fountains, the dwellings of the priests, and sometimes arsenals; since each house of a Mexican divinity, like the ancient temple of Baal Berith, burnt by Abimelech, was a strong place. A great staircase led to the top of the truncated pyramid, and on the summit of the platform were one or two chapels, built like towers, which contained the colossal idols of the divinity, to whom the Teocalli was dedicated. This part of the edifice must be considered as the most consecrated place; like the ναος, or rather the σηκος, of the Grecian temples. It was there also, that the priests kept up the sacred fire. From the peculiar construction of the edifice we have just described, the priest who offered the sacrifice was seen by a great mass of the people at the same time; the procession of the *teopixqui*, ascending or descending the staircase of the pyramid, was beheld at a considerable distance. The inside of the edifice was the burial place of the kings and principal personages of Mexico. It is impossible to read the descriptions, which Herodotus and Diodorus Siculus have left us of the temple of Jupiter Belus, without being struck with the resemblance of that Babylonian monument to the Teocallis of Anahuac.

"At the period when the Mexicans, or Aztecks, one of the seven tribes of the Anahuatlacks, (inhabitants of the banks of rivers,) took possession, in the year 1190, of the equinoctial region of New Spain, they already found the pyramidal monuments of Teotihuacan, of Cholula, or Cholollan, and of Papantla. They attributed these great edifices to the Toltecks, a powerful and civilized nation, who inhabited Mexico five hundred years earlier, who made use of hieroglyphical characters, who computed the year more precisely, and had a more exact chronology than the greater part of the people of the old continent. The Aztecks knew not with certainty what tribe had inhabited the country of Anahuac before the Toltecks; and consequently the belief, that the houses of the deity of Teotihuacan and of Cholollan was the work of the Toltecks, assigned them the highest antiquity they could conceive. It is however possible, that they might have been constructed before the invasion of the Toltecks; that is, before the year 648 of the vulgar era. We ought not to be astonished, that no history of any American nation should precede the seventh century; and that the annals of the Toltecks should be as uncertain as those of the Pelasgi and the Ausonians. The learned Mr. Schloezer has clearly proved, that the history of the north of Europe reaches no higher than the tenth century, an epocha when Mexico was in a more advanced state of civilization than Denmark, Sweden and Russia.

"The Teocalli of Mexico was dedicated to Tezcatlipolica, the first of the Azteck divinities after Teotl, who is the supreme and invisible Being;

and to Huitzilopochtli, the God of war. It was built by the Aztecks, on the model of the pyramids of Teotihuacan, six years only before the discovery of America by Christopher Columbus. This truncated pyramid, called by Cortez the principal temple, was ninetyseven metres in breadth at its basis, and nearly fiftyfour metres in height. It is not astonishing, that a building of these dimensions should have been destroyed a few years after the siege of Mexico. In Egypt there scarcely remain any vestiges of the enormous pyramids, which towered amidst the waters of the lake Mœris, and which Herodotus says were ornamented with colossal statues. The pyramids of Porsenna, of which the description seems somewhat fabulous, and four of which, according to Varro, were more than eighty metres in height, have equally disappeared in Etruria.*

"But if the European conquerors overthrew the Teocallis of the Aztecks, they did not alike succeed in destroying more ancient monuments, that are attributed to the Tolteck nation. We shall give a succinct description of these monuments, remarkable for their form and magnitude.

"The group of the pyramids of Teotihuacan is in the valley of Mexico, eight leagues northeast from the capital, in a plain that bears the name of Micoatl, or the *Path of the Dead*. There are two large pyramids dedicated to the Sun (Tonatiuh,) and to the Moon (Meztli); and these are surrounded by several hundreds of small pyramids, which form streets

* Plin. xxxvi. 19.

in exact lines from north to south, and from east to west. Of these two great Teocallis, one is fiftyfive the other fortyfour metres in perpendicular height. The basis of the first is two hundred and eight metres in length; whence it results, that the Tonatiuh Yztaqual, according to Mr. Oteyza's measurement, made in 1803, is higher than the Mycerinus, or third of the three great pyramids of Geeza in Egypt, and the length of its base nearly equal to that of the Cephren. The small pyramids, which surround the great houses of the Sun and the Moon, are scarcely nine or ten metres high; and served, according to the tradition of the natives, as burial places for the chiefs of the tribes. Around the Cheops and the Mycerinus in Egypt, there are eight small pyramids, placed with symmetry, and parallel to the fronts of the greater. The two Teocallis of Teotihuacan had four principal stories, each of which was subdivided into steps, the edges of which are still to be distinguished. The nucleus is composed of clay mixed with small stones, and it is encased by a thick wall of tezontli, or porous amygdaloid.* This construction recals to mind that of one of the Egyptian pyramids of Sakharah, which has six stories; and which, according to Pocock, is a mass of pebbles and yellow mortar, covered on the outside with rough stones. On the top of the great Mexican Teocallis were two colossal statues of the Sun, and the Moon: they were of stone, and covered with plates of gold, of which they were stripped by the soldiers of Cortez.—

* Mandelstein of the German mineralogists.

When bishop Zumaraga, a Franciscan monk, undertook the destruction of whatever related to the worship, the history, and the Antiquities of the natives of America, he ordered also the demolition of the idols of the plain of Micoatl. We still discover the remains of a staircase built with large hewn stone, which formerly led to the platform of the Teocalli.

"On the east of the group of the pyramids of Teotihuacan, on descending the Cordillera towards the Gulph of Mexico, in a thick forest, called Tajin, rises the pyramid of Papantla. This monument was by chance discovered scarcely thirty years ago, by some Spanish hunters; for the Indians carefully conceal from the whites whatever was an object of ancient veneration. The form of this Teocalli, which had six, perhaps seven stories, is more tapering than that of any other monument of this kind; it is nearly eighteen metres in height, while the breadth of its basis is only twentyfive. This small edifice is built entirely with hewn stones, of an extraordinary size, and very beautifully and regularly shaped. Three staircases lead to the top. The covering of its steps is decorated with hieroglyphical sculpture, and small niches, which are arranged with great symmetry. The number of these niches seems to allude to the three hundred and eighteen simple and compound signs of the days of the Cempohualilhuitl, or civil calendar of the Toltecks.

"The greatest, most ancient, and most celebrated of the whole of the pyramidal monuments of Anahuac is the Teocalli of Cholula. It is called in the

PLATE VII.

Engraved for the American Antiquarian Society.

A VIEW OF THE PYRAMID OF CHOLULA, NEAR MEXICO.

present day the Mountain made by the hand of Man *(monte hecho a manos.)** At a distance it has the aspect of a natural hill covered with vegetation.†

"A vast plain, the Puebla, is separated from the valley of Mexico by the chain of volcanic mountains, which extend from Popocatepetl, towards Rio Frio, and the peak of Telapon. This plain, fertile though destitute of trees, is rich in memorials, interesting to Mexican history. In it flourished the capitals of the three republicks of Tlascalla, Huexocingo and Cholula, which, notwithstanding their continual dissensions, resisted with no less firmness the despotism and usurping spirit of the Azteck kings.

"The small city of Cholula, which Cortez, in his Letters to Charles V. compares with the most populous cities of Spain, contains at present scarcely sixteen thousand inhabitants. The pyramid is to the east of the city, on the road which leads from Cholula to Puebla. It is well preserved on the western side, which is that represented in the engraving.— The plain of Cholula presents that aspect of barrenness, which is peculiar to plains elevated two thousand two hundred metres above the level of the

---

* The pyramid of Cholula bore also the names of Toltecatl, Ecaticpac, and Tlachihuatepetl. I presume, that this last denomination is derived from the Mexican verb *tlachiani*, to see around oneself, and *tepetl*, a mountain; because the Teocalli served as a watch tower, to reconnoitre the approach of an enemy in the wars, which were perpetually occurring between the Cholulains and the inhabitants of Tlascala.

† This pyramid is represented by the annexed plate, in its present ruined state, from a drawing by Humboldt.

ocean. A few plants of the agave and dracæna rise on the foreground, and at a distance the summit of the volcano of Orizaba is beheld covered with snow; a colossal mountain, five thousand two hundred and ninetyfive metres of absolute height, and of which I have published a sketch in my Mexican Atlas, plate 17.

"The Teocalli of Cholula has four stories, all of equal height. It appears to have been constructed exactly in the direction of the four cardinal points; but as the edges of the stories are not very distinct, it is difficult to ascertain their primitive direction. This pyramidical monument has a broader basis than that of any other edifice of the same kind in the old continent. I measured it carefully, and ascertained, that its perpendicular height is only fifty metres, but that each side of its basis is four hundred and thirtynine metres in length. Torquemada computes its height at seventyseven metres; Betancourt, at sixtyfive; and Clavigero, at sixtyone. Bernal Diaz del Castillo, a common soldier in the army of Cortez, amused himself by counting the steps of the staircases, which led to the platform of the Teocallis; he found one hundred and fourteen in the great temple of Tenochtitlan, one hundred and seventeen in that of Tezcuco, and one hundred and twenty in that of Cholula. The basis of the pyramid of Cholula is twice as broad as that of Cheops; but its height is very little more than that of the pyramid of Mycerinus. On comparing the dimensions of the house of the Sun, at Teotihuacan, with those of the pyramid of Cholula, we see, that the people, who constructed these remarkable monuments, intended to give them the same height, but with bases, the length of which should be in the proportion of one to two. We find also a considerable difference in the proportions between the base and the height in these various monuments; in the three great pyramids of Geeza, the heights are to the bases as 1 to 1.7; in the pyramid of Papantla covered with hieroglyphicks, this ratio is as 1 to 1.4; in the great pyramid of Teotihuacan, as 1 to 3.7; and in that of Cholula as 1 to 7.8. This last monument is built with unbaked bricks *(xamilli,)* alternating with layers of clay.— I have been assured by some Indians of Cholula, that the inside is hollow; and that, during the abode of Cortez in this city, their ancestors had concealed, in the body of the pyramid, a considerable number of warriours, who were to fall suddenly on the Spaniards; but the materials with which the Teocalli is built, and the silence of the historians of those times,* give but little probability to this assertion.

"It is certain, however, that in the interiour of this pyramid, as in other Teocallis, there are considerable cavities, which were used as sepulchres for the natives. A particular circumstance led to this discovery. Seven or eight years ago, the road from Puebla to Mexico, which before passed to the north of the pyramid, was changed. In tracing the road, the first story was cut through, so that an eighth part remained isolated like a heap of bricks. In making this opening a square house was discovered in the interiour of the pyramid, built of stone, and supported by beams made of the wood of the

---

* Cartas de Hernan Cortez; Mexico 1770, p. 69.

deciduous cypress (cupressus disticha.) The house contained two skeletons, idols in basalt, and a great number of vases, curiously varnished and painted. No pains were taken to preserve these objects, but it is said to have been carefully ascertained, that this house, covered with bricks and strata of clay, had no outlet. Supposing that the pyramid was built, not by the Toltecks, the first inhabitants of Cholula, but by prisoners made by the Cholulans from the neighbouring nations, it is possible, that they were the carcasses of some unfortunate slaves, who had been shut up to perish in the interiour of the Teocalli. We examined the remains of this subterraneous house, and observed a particular arrangement of the bricks, tending to diminish the pressure made on the roof. The natives being ignorant of the manner of making arches, placed very large bricks horizontally, so that the upper course should pass beyond the lower. The continuation of this kind of stepwork served in some measure as a substitute for the Gothic vault, and similar vestiges have been found in several Egyptian edifices. An adit dug through the Teocalli of Cholula, to examine its internal structure, would be an interesting operation; and it is singular, that the desire of discovering hidden treasure has not prompted the undertaking.— During my travels in Peru, in visiting the vast ruins of the city of Chimu, near Mansiche, I went into the interiour of the famous Huaca de Toledo, the tomb of a Peruvian prince, in which Garci Gutierez de Toledo discovered, on digging a gallery, in 1576, massive gold amounting in value to more than five millions of francs, as is proved by the book of accounts, preserved in the mayor's office at Truxillo.

"The great Teocalli of Cholula, called also the *Mountain of unbaked bricks* (tlalchihualtepec,) had an altar on its top, dedicated to Quetzalcoatl, the god of the air. This Quetzalcoatl, whose name signifies serpent clothed with green feathers, from *coatl*, serpent, and *quetzalli*, green feathers, is the most mysterious being of the whole Mexican mythology. He was a white and bearded man, like the Bochica of the Muyscas, of whom we spoke in our descriptions of the Cataract of Tequendama.— He was high priest of Tula (Tollan,) legislator, chief of a religious sect, which, like the Sonyasis and the Bouddhists of Indostan, inflicted on themselves the most cruel penances. He introduced the custom of piercing the lips and the ears, and lacerating the rest of the body with the prickles of the agave leaves, or the thorns of the cactus; and of putting reeds into the wounds, in order that the blood might be seen to trickle more copiously. In a Mexican drawing in the Vatican library,* I have seen a figure representing Quetzalcoatl appeasing by his penance the wrath of the gods, when, thirteen thousand and sixty years after the creation of the World, (I follow the very vague chronology computed by Rios) a great famine prevailed in the province of Culan. The saint had chosen his place of retirement near Tlaxapuchicalco, on the volcano Catcitepetl *(Speaking Mountain,)* where he walked barefooted on agave leaves armed with prickles.

---

* Codex anonymous, No. 3738, fol. 8.

We seem to behold one of those rishi, hermits of the Ganges, whose pious austerity* is celebrated in the Pouranas.

"The reign of Quetzalcoatl was the golden age of the people of Anahuac. At that period, all animals, and even men, lived in peace; the earth brought forth, without culture, the most fruitful harvests; and the air was filled with a multitude of birds, which were admired for their song, and the beauty of their plumage. But this reign, like that of Saturn, and the happiness of the world, were not of long duration; the great spirit Tezcatlipoca, the Brahma of the nations of Anahuac, offered Quetzalcoatl a beverage, which, in rendering him immortal, inspired him with a taste for travelling; and particularly with an irresistible desire of visiting a distant country, called by tradition Tlapallan.† The resemblance of this name to that of Huehuetlapallan, the country of the Toltecks, appears not to be accidental. But how can we conceive, that this white man, priest of Tula, should have taken his direction, as we shall presently find, to the southeast, towards the plains of Cholula, and thence to the eastern coasts of Mexico, in order to visit this northern country, whence his ancestors had issued in the five hundred and ninetysixth year of our era?

"Quetzalcoatl, in crossing the territory of Cholula, yielded to the entreaties of the inhabitants, who offered him the reins of government. He dwelt twenty years among them, taught them to cast

---

* Schlegel über Sprache and Weisheit der Indier, p. 132.
† Clavigero Storia di Messico, tom. 2, p. 12.

metals, ordered fasts of eight days, and regulated the intercalations of the Tolteck year. He preached peace to men, and would permit no other offerings to the Divinity, than the first fruits of the harvest. From Cholula, Quetzalcoatl passed on to the mouth of the river Goasacoalco, where he disappeared, after having declared to the Cholulans (Chololtecatles,) that he would return in a short time to govern them again, and renew their happiness.

"It was the posterity of this saint, whom the unhappy Montezuma thought he recognized in the soldiers of Cortez. "We know by our books," said he, in his first interview with the Spanish General, "that myself, and those who inhabit this country, are not natives, but strangers, who came from a great distance. We know also, that the chief, who led our ancestors hither, returned for a certain time to his primitive country, and thence came back to seek those, who were here established. He found them married to the women of this land, having a numerous posterity, and living in cities, which they had built. Our ancestors hearkened not to their ancient master, and he returned alone. We have always believed, that his descendants would one day come to take possession of this country. Since you arrive from that region, where the Sun rises, and, as you assure me, you have long known us, I cannot doubt, but that the king, who sends you, is our natural master."*

* First Letter of Cortez, § 21 and 29.

"The size of the platform of the pyramid of Cholula, on which I made a great number of astronomical observations, is four thousand two hundred square metres. From it the eye ranges over a magnificent prospect; Popocatepetl, Iztaccihuatl, the peak of Orizaba, and the Sierra de Tlascalla, famous for the tempests which gather around its summit. We view at the same time three mountains higher than Mount Blanc, two of which are still burning volcanoes. A small chapel, surrounded with cypress, and dedicated to the Virgin de los Remedios, has succeeded to the temple of the god of the air, or the Mexican Indra. An ecclesiastick of the Indian race celebrates mass every day on the top of this antique monument.

"In the time of Cortez, Cholula was considered as a holy city. No where existed a greater number of Teocallis, of priests, and religious orders *(tlamacazque;)* no spot displayed greater magnificence in the celebration of publick worship, or more austerity in its penances and fasts. Since the introduction of Christianity among the Indians, the symbols of a new worship have not entirely effaced the remembrance of the old. The people assemble in crowds, from distant quarters, at the summit of the pyramid, to celebrate the festival of the Virgin. A mysterious dread, a religious awe, fills the soul of the Indian at the sight of this immense pile of bricks, covered with shrubs and perpetual verdure.

"When we consider in the same point of view the pyramidical monuments of Egypt, of Asia, and of the New Continent, we see, that, though their form is alike, their destination was altogether different. The group of pyramids at Geeza and at Sakhara in Egypt; the triangular pyramid of the Queen of the Scythians, Zarina, which was a stadium high, and three in circumference, and which was decorated with a colossal figure;* the fourteen Etruscan pyramids, which are said to have been enclosed in the labyrinth of the king Porsenna, at Clusium; were reared to serve as the sepulchres of the illustrious dead. Nothing is more natural to men, than to commemorate the spot where rest the ashes of those, whose memory they cherish; whether it be, as in the infancy of the race, by simple mounds of earth, or in later periods by the towering height of the tumulus. Those of the Chinese and of Thibet have only a few metres of elevation.† Farther to the west the dimensions increase; the tumulus of the king Alyattes, father of Crœsus, in Lydia, was six stadia, and that of Ninus was more than ten stadia in diameter.‡ In the north of Europe the sepulchres of the Scandinavian king Gormus, and the queen Daneboda, covered with mounds of earth, are three hundred metres broad, and more than thirty high. We meet with these tumuli in both hemispheres; in Virginia, and in Canada, as well as in Peru, where numerous galleries, built with stone, and communicating with each other by shafts, fill up the interiour of the *huacas*, or artificial hills. In Asia these rustick monuments

* Diodorus Siculus, lib. 2, c. 34.

† Duhalde, Description of China, tom. 2, p. 126. Asiatic Researches, vol. ii. p. 314.

‡ Herodotus, lib. 1, c. 93. Ctesias, apud Diod. Sicul. lib. 2, c. 7.

have been decorated with the refinement of eastern luxury, while their primitive forms have been preserved. The tombs of Pergamus are cones of earth, raised on a circular wall, which seems to have been encased with marble.*

"The Teocallis, or Mexican pyramids, were at once temples and tombs. We have already observed, that the plain, on which were built the houses of the Sun and of the Moon at Teotihuaca, is called the *Path of the Dead;* but the essential and principal part of a Teocalli was the chapel, the *naos,* at the top of the edifice. In the infancy of civilization, high places were chosen by the people to offer sacrifices to the gods. The first altars, the first temples, were erected on mountains; and when these mountains were isolated, the worshippers delighted in the toil of shaping them into regular forms, cutting them by stories, and making stairs to reach the summit more easily. Both continents afford numerous examples of these hills divided into terraces, and supported by walls of brick or stone. The Teocallis appear to me to be merely artificial hills, raised in the midst of a plain, and intended to serve as a basis to the altars. What more sublime and awful than a sacrifice, that is offered in the sight of an assembled nation! The pagods of Indostan have nothing in common with the Mexican temples. That of Tanjore, of which Mr. Daniell has given beautiful drawings,† is a

* Choiseul Gouffier, Voyage Pittoresque de la Grèce, tom. 2, p. 27 to 31.

† Oriental Scenery, Pl. 17.

tower with several stories, but the altar is not at the top of the monument.

"The pyramid of Bel was at once the temple and tomb of this god. Strabo does not speak of this monument as a temple, he simply calls it the tomb of Belus. In Arcadia, the tumulus ($\chi\tilde{\omega}\mu\alpha$,) which contained the ashes of Calisto, bore on its top a temple of Diana. Pausanias* describes it as a cone, made by the hands of man, and long covered with vegetation. This is a very remarkable monument, in which the temple is only an incidental decoration; it serves, if we may use the expression, as an intermediary step between the pyramids of Sakhara and the Mexican Teocallis."

* Pausanias, lib. 8, c. 35.